Start

a Career

as

a Life Coach

START A CAREER

AS A LIFE COACH

Comprehensive Educational Guide to learning

Skills and Techniques of Coaching

Made by

RENÉ LAURITSEN

Published by

VIRTUS

Table of Contents

PART I

FOUNDATIONS OF LIFE COACHING

Your Gateway to Impacting Lives Starts Here!

Do you feel the call to guide, inspire, and uplift others to their highest potential? If so, the incredible journey to becoming a certified life coach begins with laying the right foundation.

Introducing Part I of our comprehensive guidebook: "Foundations of Life Coaching."

What Will I Learn?

> » What Exactly is Life Coaching?
> » Get past the buzzwords and dive deep into what life coaching truly entails. Learn how this empowering profession distinguishes itself from therapy, mentoring, and consulting.
> » The Rich Tapestry of Coaching History

> » How did life coaching become the influential industry it is today? We take you on a riveting ride through its origins, drawing from psychology, business consulting, and even the self-help movement.
> » Unlock the Psychology Behind Coaching
> » Arm yourself with the psychological theories that are the bedrock of effective coaching. Understanding the "why" behind the "how" will make you an unparalleled guide in your clients' journeys.

Why Should I Care?

Understanding the foundational theories and principles behind life coaching is like building a house on solid ground. It equips you to:

> » Navigate Complex Emotions: Gain the tools to help your clients tackle their most intricate emotional challenges.
> » Make Informed Decisions: Ground your coaching practice in proven psychological theories and methods.
> » Elevate Your Coaching: A nuanced understanding of the field will set you apart from the competition and help you offer a truly transformative experience to your clients.

Get Ready to Transform Lives, Starting with Yours!

By diving into this book, you're not just learning; you're taking the first step in a lifelong journey to empower others—and yourself. Are you ready to change lives? Your own transformation begins here!

CHAPTER 1

WHAT IS LIFE COACHING?

Have you ever wondered what it takes to help someone transform their life? Or perhaps you've heard the term "life coaching" tossed around but aren't quite sure what it means?

Dive into the exhilarating world of life coaching and uncover its true essence. Move past the myths and misconceptions and discover how this incredible profession stands apart from therapy, consulting, and mentoring. Learn about the scope, limitations, and the undeniable impact a life coach can have on individuals and society at large.

Get ready for an eye-opening introduction that will not only define life coaching for you but will also lay the cornerstone for your future career in transforming lives, including your own!

History of Life Coaching

While the concept of guiding others toward their personal and professional goals may seem timeless, life coaching as a distinct profession has a fascinating history worth exploring. This enriching journey will provide you with context, helping you understand not only where life coaching came from but also where it's headed.

Life coaching was born from a blend of disciplines—psychology, business consulting, counseling, and even elements from spirituality and self-help movements. From its early days in the 1960s, where it was often viewed as a subset of organizational psychology, to its rapid proliferation in the late 20th and early 21st centuries, life coaching has established itself as an independent field of practice, complete with its own techniques, ethical guidelines, and certification programs.

Understanding this history will not only deepen your respect for the profession but will also enhance your ability to navigate its complexities. As you move forward on your journey to becoming a life coach, the historical backdrop will serve as a constant reminder of the depth and breadth of the field you're entering, inspiring you to be a part of its exciting future.

Various Forms of Coaching

Life coaching is a multifaceted profession that can transform lives in a plethora of ways. Whether it's about achieving work-life balance, climbing the corporate ladder, or embracing a healthier lifestyle, life coaching has specialized areas to meet diverse needs. Let's delve into some of the primary forms of coaching you might encounter or decide to specialize in:

Personal Life Coaching

This form of coaching primarily addresses personal goals, life balance, and general well-being. It can cover everything from helping someone achieve work-life balance, improve relationships, or build self-esteem. Personal life coaches often serve as a confidante and guide, helping clients navigate challenges and realize their full potential.

Career Coaching

Geared towards professional development, this specialized area focuses on aiding clients in career transitions, job searches, and professional growth. A career coach can help clients identify their strengths and weaknesses, create actionable career plans, and offer guidance through job interviews, promotions, or even career changes.

Health and Wellness Coaching

This approach is centered around physical health and lifestyle choices. Health and wellness coaches guide clients towards achieving their health-related goals, whether it's weight loss, improved physical performance, or managing a chronic condition. This type of coaching often overlaps with nutritional counseling and exercise planning.

Additional Forms

While the above are the primary categories, there are also niche forms of coaching that cater to specific needs, including but not limited to:

» Financial Coaching: Guiding clients towards financial stability and growth
» Relationship Coaching: Aimed at improving interpersonal relationships

As you continue your journey in becoming a life coach, understanding these various forms can help you find your niche, allowing you to offer targeted and effective coaching experiences to your future clients.

What's the Objectives of Life Coaching?

Life coaching is more than just a conversation; it's a transformative journey driven by specific objectives. But what exactly are these goals, and how do they help both the coach and the coachee?

- » *Clarity and Direction:* One of the fundamental objectives of life coaching is to help individuals gain clarity about their aspirations, desires, and concerns. By defining clear goals, clients can craft a more focused and intentional path forward.

- » *Self-awareness:* Life coaching prompts introspection. It's about helping individuals recognize their strengths, weaknesses, beliefs, and values, allowing them to better understand who they are and how they interact with the world around them.

- » *Accountability:* A life coach serves as an accountability partner, ensuring that individuals remain committed to their goals and take consistent action towards achieving them.

- » *Skill Development:* From communication and decision-making to emotional intelligence and resilience, life coaching aids in refining various personal and professional skills.

- » *Overcoming Barriers:* Every journey has its obstacles. Life coaches assist in identifying these barriers—be they mental blocks, past traumas, or external challenges—and crafting strategies to navigate or overcome them.

- » *Empowerment:* At its core, life coaching is about empowerment. It's about giving individuals the tools, strategies, and confidence to take control of their lives, to drive their own change, and to achieve their desired outcomes.

By pursuing these objectives, life coaching doesn't just offer solutions to immediate problems; it cultivates a mindset of growth, resilience, and continuous self-improvement. The journey with a life coach is about unveiling one's full potential and, most importantly, learning how to harness it for a brighter and more fulfilling future.

CHAPTER 2

WHY BECOME A LIFE COACH?

Do you have an innate desire to help others, but you're not quite sure how to transform that drive into a fulfilling career? Does the idea of flexibility, income potential, and deep-rooted career satisfaction sound like the professional trifecta you've been seeking? If so, you may be standing at the threshold of an incredibly rewarding career pathway. Welcome to Chapter 2, where we explore the multi-faceted benefits of becoming a life coach.

Delve into the profound impact you can have on people's lives while also enjoying the freedom and financial benefits this versatile career offers. Discover how life coaching can be a win-win, enriching not only your clients' worlds but also your own personal and financial life.

We'll uncover the tangible and intangible rewards—whether it's the income potential that allows you to live comfortably or the career satisfaction that comes from seeing your clients thrive.

By the end of this chapter, you'll see how becoming a life coach is not just a career but a calling—one that brings together purpose, skill, and the potential for both financial and emotional rewards.

Personal Benefits: The Heart of the Coaching Experience

The art of life coaching often takes place in the quiet moments—the pause in conversation when realization dawns, the softening of a client's eyes when they discover a new perspective, or the joyous "a-ha" moment when a seemingly insurmountable obstacle is finally conquered. In these transformative instances, you earn something far more valuable than any financial currency: the soulful currency of making a genuine difference in another human being's life.

As a life coach, you serve as a catalyst for change, helping clients transition from where they are to where they aspire to be. While it's their journey, the satisfaction and fulfillment you gain from playing a role in it are immeasurable. Each coaching session is not just a meeting but an opportunity for a life-altering shift. Whether it's helping a client achieve a career milestone, guiding them towards improved relationships, or assisting them in self-discovery, the rewards ripple far beyond the coaching room.

Your positive impact echoes in the lives of the people you help, extending to their families, communities, and even generations. The act of facilitating growth in others often sparks growth within yourself, both personally and professionally, making it one of the most gratifying aspects of the job.

For many, the fulfillment derived from helping others is the very lifeblood of their coaching practice. The 'feel-good' factor has a lasting effect, nourishing your soul and invigorating your practice with a sense of purpose that few other professions can offer.

In life coaching, each thank-you note, each grateful smile, each personal milestone reached, becomes a bead on the string of your career's satisfaction necklace—a tangible reminder of why you chose this path and the indelible impact you have on the world.

Professional Benefits: The Tangible Rewards of a Life Coach's Journey

Many people are drawn to life coaching by the prospect of making a meaningful difference in others' lives. However, the financial aspect cannot be ignored, and thankfully, life coaching offers an avenue for both. With the increasing recognition of the value that a skilled life coach brings, the demand—and therefore the income potential—is significant. Whether you are in private practice or part of a larger coaching organization, the opportunity for a prosperous career is compelling. Some coaches even opt for specialized niches, such as executive coaching or health coaching, which can further increase earning potential.

But financial rewards in life coaching are not merely transactional; they're a reflection of the expertise, dedication, and impact you bring to your clients' lives. Many find that as they refine their skills and expand their client base, the financial benefits follow naturally, allowing for a comfortable lifestyle and the freedom to invest back into their practice and personal development.

Career Satisfaction: More Than Just a Job

In many professions, the equation of success often omits one crucial element: job satisfaction. Life coaching, however, fills this gap in a profound way. The work you do isn't just a series of tasks; it's a vocation filled with purpose. You'll find that the challenges you help clients overcome translate into intrinsic rewards that are deeply fulfilling. Each day brings new opportunities for both you and your clients to grow, learn, and thrive.

The sense of achievement that comes from helping someone break through barriers or reach new heights in their personal or professional life is incomparable. This joy is further amplified when your clients achieve long-term success, proving the enduring value of your coaching. Your satisfaction isn't just found in the milestones but in the journey—each step forward marks not just your client's progress but your own growth as a skilled and empathetic coach.

In essence, life coaching offers a career where the professional rewards are as enriching as the personal ones, making it a holistic path that caters to multiple facets of your well-being.

CHAPTER 3

LIFE COACHING VS. OTHER HELPING PROFESSIONS

Life coaching often gets confused with other helping professions like therapy or consulting.

The realm of personal and professional development has expanded significantly over the years. Within this spectrum, life coaching, therapy, and consulting emerge as prominent helping professions.

However, they are distinct in their approach, goals, and methodologies. Understanding these distinctions is crucial for anyone looking to hire a professional in these areas or considering a career in one of them.

Life Coaching

Focus: Life coaching primarily revolves around the present and the future. It emphasizes helping clients identify their goals, overcome present-day challenges, and move towards desired future outcomes.

Method: Life coaches employ a partnership model, working alongside clients as they discover solutions and strategies tailored to their unique circumstances. This is a collaborative process, with the coach serving as a facilitator and accountability partner.

Goal: The primary aim is to empower clients to take actionable steps towards achieving their personal or professional goals, offering them tools and strategies to navigate life's challenges with confidence.

Therapy (or Counseling)

Focus: Therapy, often referred to as counseling, typically deals with healing past traumas, understanding emotional concerns, and managing psychological disorders.

Method: Therapists are trained to diagnose and treat various emotional and psychological issues. Their methods might include cognitive-behavioral techniques, psychodynamic approaches, or other therapeutic modalities.

Goal: The primary objective is to provide clients with a safe space to process emotions, heal from past traumas, and develop coping mechanisms to handle emotional or psychological challenges.

Consulting

Focus: Consulting usually targets a specific problem or challenge within an organization or individual's professional sphere. It's more industry-specific and less holistic than life coaching.

Method: Consultants are experts in particular fields or areas, providing specialized guidance and advice. They assess situations, offer solutions, and may even implement those solutions on behalf of the client.

Goal: The central aim is to improve a specific aspect of a business or professional practice, be it in areas like operations, management, or strategy. Consultants offer a roadmap to address these specific challenges and enhance efficiency or profitability.

In Summary:

While there is some overlap among life coaching, therapy, and consulting, it's essential to understand their distinct methodologies and aims. Life coaching is about empowerment and future-focused action. Therapy delves deeper into emotional healing and past experiences. Consulting zeroes in on specialized professional challenges with an expert's perspective.

Recognizing these distinctions not only provides clarity for potential clients but also ensures that those seeking help choose the most appropriate avenue for their needs. For those considering a career in one of these fields, understanding these nuances is paramount in aligning one's passion, skills, and the desired impact in their chosen profession.

What Sets Life Coaching Apart

Navigating the landscape of helping professions can be like walking through a maze; the boundaries sometimes appear blurred. Life coaching, however, presents distinct attributes that set it apart from its professional counterparts like therapy and consulting. Understanding these unique facets is essential for would-be coaches and clients alike.

Future-Focused: Planning the Steps Ahead, Not Just Looking Back

One of the most striking differences between life coaching and therapy is the focus on the future. While therapy often provides a safe space to explore past experiences, emotional issues, and unresolved traumas, life coaching propels you forward.

In a life coaching engagement, you work on laying out tangible steps to reach specific life or career goals. Whether it's launching a business, improving interpersonal relationships, or achieving work-life balance, the emphasis is squarely on actionable strategies to create the future you envision.

This future-orientation does not mean that life coaching ignores the past; rather, it uses the past as a reference point, not a dwelling place.

Client-Led: You're the Expert on Your Life

Another unique feature of life coaching is its client-led approach. Unlike consulting, where a consultant analyzes a problem and provides expert solutions, life coaching operates on the belief that you are the expert of your own life. The life coach's role is not to give you the answers but to ask the right questions.

In each session, the client sets the agenda. What topics are most pressing? What challenges are you currently facing? What progress has been made toward goals? This process ensures that the client's needs and objectives are at the forefront, making each coaching session as relevant and impactful as possible.

The client-led approach empowers individuals to take charge of their destiny. It fosters self-reliance and encourages accountability. You are not just passively absorbing advice; you are actively involved in crafting your path forward.

Life coaching stands apart as a future-focused and client-led profession. These attributes make it an empowering avenue for individuals looking to take actionable steps toward their future goals while remaining the expert of their own lives. Whether you are a prospective client seeking guidance or an aspiring coach wanting to make an impact, understanding what sets life coaching apart will help you make an informed decision in your personal or professional journey.

CHAPTER 4

KEY SKILLS AND ATTRIBUTES OF A LIFE COACH

Ever wondered what it takes to be a transformative life coach who creates lasting impact? Chapter 4 is your roadmap to the essential skills and attributes that set great coaches apart. Whether you're a seasoned professional or just getting started, learn the art of active listening, the power of empathy, and the secrets to effective communication. Dive into the toolkit every coach needs, not just to survive but to thrive in this rewarding career.

Topics in this chapter include:

- » Active Listening: The art of fully engaging with the client's words and underlying emotions.
- » Empathy: The ability to understand and share the feelings of others.
- » Communication: The knack for conveying ideas and concepts clearly.
- » Problem-solving: Guiding clients to find their own solutions to issues.

> » Goal-setting: Helping clients set achievable, realistic goals.

Active Listening: The Art of Fully Engaging with the Client's Words and Underlying Emotions

Active listening is not just about hearing; it's about understanding. As a life coach, your ability to listen actively could mean the difference between a transformative coaching session and an ineffective one. In active listening, you're not just waiting for your turn to speak; you're fully engaged with what the client is saying and what they're not saying. You're paying attention to the words, the pauses, the tone of voice, and the emotions underlying those words.

Why Active Listening Matters

In life coaching, the relationship you build with your client is the cornerstone of progress. Building trust and rapport hinges on your ability to show the client that they are heard, understood, and valued. Active listening fosters this relationship and provides you with critical information you'll use to guide the coaching process.

The Components of Active Listening

Verbal Acknowledgement: Use affirmative words like "I see," "I understand," or "Tell me more" to let your client know you are with them.

Non-verbal cues: Your body language can communicate attentiveness. Eye contact, nodding, and leaning in slightly can all demonstrate that you are engaged.

Questioning: Use open-ended questions to encourage the client to expand on their thoughts.

Paraphrasing: Repeat back what you've heard in your own words, asking for clarification to ensure you've understood correctly.

Emotional Tuning: Be attuned to shifts in tone, pace, and body language as these can give you insights into the client's emotional state.

Exercise: The "Pause and Reflect" Technique

Objective: To strengthen active listening by pausing to reflect on what the speaker is saying before giving a response.

1. Pair Up: Designate one person as the "Speaker" and the other as the "Listener."

2. Topic Selection: The Speaker should select a topic that is meaningful but not overly complex. The objective here is to focus on the listening, not necessarily problem-solving.

3. The Rule of Pause: In this exercise, the Listener must pause for at least five seconds after the Speaker stops talking. Use this time to truly absorb what was said, to understand the emotion behind the words, and to formulate an empathetic and thoughtful response.

4. Reflect and Respond: After the pause, the Listener should reflect back what they heard in a manner that shows understanding and empathy. For instance, if the Speaker says, "I was overwhelmed with work today," the Listener might respond, "It sounds like today was really stressful for you, with a lot on your plate."

5. Switch and Continue: After a few turns, swap roles so both participants get the experience of active listening.

6. Discussion: Once you have both had a chance to be the Listener, discuss the experience. Did the pause make the Listener's response more thoughtful? Was the Speaker's message more deeply understood?

Key Takeaways:

» The pause allows the Listener time to fully process what the Speaker is saying, leading to a more empathetic and accurate reflection.

» The exercise teaches the value of silence in effective communication.

» It demonstrates how quick responses may sometimes miss the depth of what is being conveyed.

This exercise can be eye-opening in showing how a simple pause can elevate the quality of your listening and, by extension, the entire coaching conversation.

Active listening is a skill that takes practice, but its payoff is immense. Not only will it improve your effectiveness as a life coach, but it will also enrich your personal relationships and your understanding of yourself.

Empathy: The Cornerstone of Effective Coaching

Empathy is often cited as one of the most critical skills for any helping profession, and life coaching is no exception. At its core, empathy is the ability to understand and share the feelings of others, to "walk a mile in someone else's shoes," so to speak. It enables a life coach to build a genuine rapport with clients, creating a safe and trustful environment where real progress can happen.

The Importance of Empathy in Life Coaching

» Guided Action: A deep understanding of a client's emotional landscape allows a coach to tailor advice and action plans that resonate with the client, increasing the likelihood of meaningful change.

» Conflict Resolution: When conflicts arise, empathy enables a coach to see the situation from the client's perspective, facilitating a resolution that honors the client's feelings and needs.

» Building Trust: Clients are more likely to open up and share their true thoughts and feelings if they sense that their coach genuinely understands and cares about them.

» Emotional Support: Life coaching isn't just about achieving goals; it's also about emotional well-being. An empathetic coach can provide emotional support that is both genuine and empowering.

The Empathy Skill Set

Being empathetic isn't just about being a "good person"—it's a skill that can be honed and developed. Effective empathetic communication includes active listening, open-ended questioning, validation, and sometimes even sharing personal stories when appropriate for establishing credibility and rapport.

While empathy is essential, it's important to remember that a coach's role is not to solve clients' problems for them. Being too emotionally involved can cloud objective judgement and even lead to burnout. Therefore, maintaining professional boundaries is crucial.

Tools and Ideas for Improving Empathy

Improving empathy is not just a philosophical endeavor but a practical one that involves specific tools and exercises. Here are some strategies to help you enhance your empathic abilities:

1. Empathy Circles

This is a structured dialogue process that allows people to speak and listen to each other in a respectful and open way. It's a great method for practicing active listening and honing your ability to understand another person's perspective.

2. Journaling

Try to write about the emotions you've observed in others, without judgment. Over time, this can help you become more aware of emotional cues and help you understand the nuances in different emotional states.

3. Emotional Intelligence Assessments

There are several online tests and tools designed to measure emotional intelligence, which includes empathy. These can be a starting point for understanding your strengths and areas for improvement.

4. Read Widely

Literature, especially fiction that dives deeply into character development, can offer insights into human psychology and the diversity of human experiences and emotions. This can be a safe space to practice putting yourself in another's shoes.

5. Practice Mindfulness

Being present in the moment allows you to engage more deeply with others. Mindfulness exercises can train you to become more aware and receptive to other people's emotions.

6. Role-Playing

A more hands-on approach can be engaging in role-playing scenarios. This practice is common in empathy training programs and can be very effective for understanding different perspectives.

7. Feedback Loop

After conversations, especially challenging ones, seek feedback on how well you listened and showed empathy. This can be an eye-opener and a crucial part of your growth process.

8. Watch and Learn

Identify people who are particularly good at displaying empathy and observe how they interact with others. You can learn a lot just by watching how they navigate conversations and handle emotional topics.

In the world of life coaching, empathy is more than just a buzzword; it's a foundational skill that can make or break your effectiveness as a coach. Mastering the art of empathy can offer you not only professional success but also personal satisfaction, as there is truly nothing like the joy of deeply connecting with another human being while helping them realize their fullest potential.

Communication: The Knack for Conveying Ideas and Concepts Clearly

As a life coach, your effectiveness hinges largely on your ability to communicate. Without clear communication, even the most brilliant insights or strategies can lose their impact. Below, we delve into the vital components of effective communication and offer exercises and tools to help you become an expert communicator.

Why Communication is Crucial in Coaching

- » *Facilitates Understanding:* A coach needs to fully understand the client's needs and aspirations, and the client, in turn, needs to understand the coach's recommendations. Clear communication makes this possible.
- » *Enhances Client Engagement:* When the client feels heard and understood, they are more likely to engage in the coaching process.
- » *Informs Decision-Making:* Good communication helps the coach and client make informed decisions based on clear, mutual understanding of the issues at hand.

Elements of Effective Communication

- » *Clarity:* Keep your language simple and straightforward. Avoid jargon unless you're certain the client understands it.
- » *Active Listening:* This is a two-way street. You need to listen as much as you speak, if not more.
- » *Empathy:* Being empathetic in your communication helps the client feel heard and understood.

Exercise: The Mirror Exercise

> » Pair up with a partner: One person plays the coach, the other plays the client.
> » Role-play a coaching scenario: The 'client' shares an issue or concern.
> » Reflect and Clarify: The 'coach' should mirror what the client says, paraphrasing their statements to confirm understanding.
> » Switch Roles: After 5 minutes, switch roles and repeat.

This exercise helps to practice not just what to say, but also how to say it, capturing the nuance and emotion behind the client's words.

Tools for Effective Communication

> » Voice Modulation Software: Software like this can analyze your tone, pitch, and speed to help you refine your spoken communication.
> » Digital Note-taking Apps: Use these to jot down key points as your client speaks, ensuring you won't forget or misinterpret what was said.
> » Customer Relationship Management (CRM) Software: Keeping track of client conversations and coaching plans can help ensure that nothing falls through the cracks.

Problem-Solving: Guiding Clients to Find Their Own Solutions to Issues

As a life coach, your role often involves guiding your clients towards solving their own problems. Unlike in other helping professions, where the expert might provide a prescribed solution, coaching empowers clients to come to their own conclusions. Below we explore why problem-solving is an essential skill in coaching, along with exercises, tools, and example questions to help you guide clients in finding their own solutions.

The Importance of Problem-Solving in Coaching

- » Client Empowerment: The aim is to make the client self-sufficient in solving future problems.
- » Personalized Solutions: When clients find their own solutions, they're more likely to be committed to the outcome.
- » Enhanced Critical Thinking: The process of problem-solving nurtures a client's critical thinking and decision-making skills.

Components of Effective Problem-Solving

- » Questioning Techniques: Use open-ended questions to facilitate thought.
- » Active Listening: Listen carefully to the client's responses to understand the crux of the problem.
- » Brainstorming: Create a safe space where any idea, no matter how outlandish, can be considered.

For example, you could start with a question like,

"What do you think is holding you back?" and follow it up with "How does that make you feel?" or "What have you tried before to solve this issue?"

Tools for Effective Problem-Solving

» Mind-Mapping Software: Utilize mind-mapping tools to visually break down a problem into its constituent parts.

» Decision Matrix: Use a decision matrix to evaluate different solutions based on a set of criteria.

» Journaling Apps: Encourage clients to jot down their thoughts, concerns, and reflections to help them better understand their problems.

Example Questions

» "Can you tell me more about the issue you're facing?"

» "What have you tried so far, and what were the results?"

» "If you could wave a magic wand and solve this problem, what would that look like?"

» "What are the potential roadblocks you foresee?"

» "What options are currently on the table for solving this problem?"

» "How would you rank these options in terms of feasibility and impact?"

» "What resources or support do you need to implement these solutions?"

» "Who else is affected by this problem, and have you considered their perspective?"

» "What are the short-term and long-term implications of each solution?"

» "What's the worst that could happen if you try one of these solutions and it fails?"

» "What criteria will you use to measure the success of a chosen solution?"

> » "How does this problem align with your broader goals or life values?"
> » "What external factors could influence the outcome of your solution?"
> » "Have you ever encountered a similar problem in the past? What did you do?"
> » "What's stopping you from implementing the best solution right now?"
> » "What steps can you take today or this week to start solving this problem?"
> » "If a friend came to you with this same problem, what advice would you give them?"
> » "Is there anyone in your network who has successfully solved a similar problem?"
> » "How committed are you, on a scale of 1-10, to solving this problem?"

Problem-solving is not just about finding a solution; it's about equipping your clients with the mental tools they need to tackle issues on their own in the future. Master this skill, and you'll not only solve problems—you'll also create more capable and self-reliant individuals.

PART II

THEORETICAL FRAMEWORKS

Ready to go beyond the basics and dive deep into the science and psychology that power successful coaching? Part II of the book, "Theoretical Frameworks," delves into the various psychological theories and models that underpin the practice of life coaching.

Topics covered will include Cognitive Behavioral Coaching, Positive Psychology, Emotional Intelligence, and the Humanistic Approach. The aim is to provide aspiring coaches with a solid grounding in the key theoretical frameworks that can guide their coaching sessions, inform their techniques, and help them understand human behavior and motivations more deeply.

Whether it's the cognitive mechanisms that influence behavior or the pillars of emotional intelligence that dictate decision-making, this section equips you with the intellectual arsenal to excel as a life coach. Transform your practice by understanding the 'why' behind the 'how.'"

CHAPTER 5

CORE THEORIES IN LIFE COACHING

Have you ever wondered what makes a coaching session effective? Or how top coaches seem to get inside their clients' heads? Chapter 5 uncovers the secret sauce—key theories that form the backbone of any successful coaching career. From Cognitive Behavioral Coaching to Humanistic and Positive Psychology, we delve into the science that will transform your intuitive skills into professional expertise.

Don't just be a life coach—be an informed life coach. Read on to equip yourself with the core theories that make all the difference. A solid theoretical foundation is crucial for any aspiring life coach. Learn about the psychological theories that inform the practice of life coaching

Positive Psychology

Positive psychology focuses on improving the quality of life and embracing strengths rather than fixing weaknesses. As a life coach, this perspective can be empowering for your clients. Positive Psychology is a branch of psychology founded by Dr. Martin Seligman that focuses on the strengths and virtues that enable individuals and communities to thrive. Unlike traditional psychological approaches that focus on treating mental illness, Positive Psychology emphasizes human strengths such as resilience, optimism, and well-being.

In life coaching, Positive Psychology can offer a robust framework for understanding what helps people flourish. Coaches employing this framework often focus on helping clients identify their strengths and leverage them to achieve specific goals or overcome challenges.

Techniques and Tools

1. Strengths Assessment

Strengths Assessment is an evaluation method that helps individuals identify their inherent abilities, talents, and skills. Various tools are available for this, such as the VIA Character Strengths Assessment, Gallup's StrengthsFinder, or below questionnaire developed for your use

During the initial sessions, coaches can encourage clients to undertake a strengths assessment. The results can become a foundation for the coaching relationship, offering targeted points for development or change. This understanding can then be used to guide clients toward goals that are aligned with their innate strengths, thereby increasing the likelihood of success and satisfaction.

The client fills out a Character Strengths questionnaire. Then the coach and the client discuss the top 5 strengths revealed and brainstorm ways to leverage them in achieving the client's goals.

Character Strengths Survey

Instructions:

Rate each statement on a scale of 1 to 5, where 1 means "Not Like Me At All" and 5 means "Very Much Like Me."

Creativity

I often come up with new and original ideas.

Rating: _______________________________________

Curiosity

I am always interested in learning something new.

Rating: _______________________________________

Open-Mindedness

I listen to other people's ideas and perspectives, even if I disagree.

Rating: _______________________________________

Love of Learning

I enjoy acquiring new skills or knowledge.

Rating: _______________________________________

Perspective

People often seek my advice because they value my point of view.

Rating: _______________________________________

Bravery

I am courageous and take risks to achieve my goals.

Rating: _______________________________________

Perseverance

I finish what I start, even when it gets tough.

Rating: ____

Integrity

I always try to be honest and true to myself.

Rating: ____

Vitality

I approach life with excitement and energy.

Rating: ____

Love

I build strong, loving relationships.

Rating: ____

Scoring:

- » 41-50: Exceptional Strengths — You possess these qualities in abundance.
- » 31-40: Strong Strengths — These are clear strengths but have room for growth.
- » 21-30: Moderate Strengths — You exhibit these traits occasionally or moderately.
- » 11-20: Emerging Strengths — These are areas for potential development.

After completing the survey, focus on your top 3-5 strengths. As a life coach, you can then help your clients understand how to leverage these strengths in achieving their life goals.

Feel free to adapt and expand upon this survey according to your coaching needs.

2. Positive Interventions

Positive interventions are exercises or activities designed to foster positive emotions, thoughts, or behaviors. These are empirically-supported tasks such as keeping a gratitude journal, performing random acts of kindness, or practicing mindfulness.

Coaches can assign these interventions as 'homework' between sessions. Clients can then discuss their experiences and insights during the next meeting. The coach can help fine-tune the interventions based on client feedback, making them more effective and personalized.

Example Exercise:

Gratitude journaling is a well-known practice, but this exercise adds an extra layer by linking gratitude to one's personal strengths.

Instructions:

- » Identify Strengths: First, have your client review their top strengths identified from the Character Strengths Survey.
- » Daily Entries: Ask your client to keep a gratitude journal for one week. Each day, they should write down things they are grateful for.
- » Link to Strengths: Here's the twist. For each entry, have your client also note which of their identified strengths helped them experience or appreciate that moment of gratitude. For example, if they're grateful for a good conversation with a friend, the strength could be "Love" or "Perspective."

» Reflect: At the end of the week, have your client review their journal. Discuss how their strengths contributed to their moments of gratitude and how they can consciously utilize these strengths more in their daily life.

This exercise is intended to not only cultivate gratitude but also to help the client become more aware of how their inherent strengths contribute to their well-being. This dual focus amplifies the benefits of the traditional gratitude journal by making it more personalized and actionable.

3. Savoring Techniques

Savoring is the conscious enjoyment of positive experiences. The act of savoring enhances the impact of a positive event by focusing attention and awareness on it.

Coaches can instruct clients on how to practice savoring in their daily lives. Whether it's enjoying a good meal, spending time with loved ones, or completing a challenging task, the practice of savoring can make good experiences even better and more memorable.

Example Exercise:

Encourage the client to choose positive experiences each week and spend five minutes relishing it. Ask them to note down the emotions they felt while savoring and discuss them in the next session.

Understanding and utilizing these techniques in your coaching practice will offer a multidimensional approach to help your clients not just solve problems but to enhance their overall quality of life.

Behavioral Theories in Life Coaching

Behavioral theories form an important cornerstone for many coaching methodologies. Rooted in the works of psychologists like B.F. Skinner, behavioral theories focus on understanding how behavior is shaped by various forms of stimuli and reinforcement.

Operant Conditioning

Operant conditioning revolves around the fundamental idea that behaviors that are reinforced tend to be repeated, while those that are punished are likely to be reduced or eliminated. This principle can be applied in a coaching setting to help clients form new habits or eliminate undesired behaviors.

For example, if a client is struggling to exercise regularly, a life coach might employ techniques derived from operant conditioning. Positive reinforcement in the form of small rewards after completing an exercise routine can encourage the client to continue with the behavior. Conversely, identifying and removing negative stimuli that discourage exercise could also be part of the strategy.

Reinforcement Schedules

Life coaches should be aware of the different schedules of reinforcement: fixed-ratio, variable-ratio, fixed-interval, and variable-interval. For example, using a variable-ratio reinforcement schedule, where rewards are given after an unpredictable number of actions, can be particularly effective in making behavior changes stick.

Social Learning Theory

Beyond the basic mechanisms of reward and punishment, social learning theory posits that individuals also learn from observing others. A coach can use this theory to model certain behaviors or to show clients videos or case studies where others have successfully implemented a desired behavior.

Techniques and Tools

- » Reward System: Create a personalized reward system for your client to reinforce positive behavior.
- » Accountability Partners: Leverage social learning theory by pairing your client with an accountability partner who is also working toward similar goals.
- » Self-Monitoring: Encourage your client to monitor their behavior, making it easier to identify triggers and patterns.

Exercise: Behavioral Contracting

Create a behavioral contract with your client, specifying the desired behavior, the form of positive reinforcement upon achieving it, and the metrics for measuring success. Review and adjust the contract as necessary during follow-up sessions.

By employing techniques and insights drawn from behavioral theories, life coaches can guide their clients through a more scientific, evidence-based approach to achieving meaningful and lasting behavior change.

Humanistic Psychology in Life Coaching

Humanistic psychology is a rich framework for life coaching, emphasizing the intrinsic goodness of individuals and the quest for self-actualization. Originating from the works of Carl Rogers and Abraham Maslow among others, this approach focuses on the individual's experience, free will, and the innate drive towards achieving one's fullest potential.

Self-Actualization

The ultimate goal in humanistic psychology, and often in life coaching, is self-actualization, which is the full realization of one's potential and talents. Life coaches utilizing a humanistic approach may aim to guide clients through the hierarchy of needs, from basic security and social needs to self-esteem, eventually culminating in self-actualization.

Unconditional Positive Regard

A core tenet of humanistic psychology is the importance of unconditional positive regard. This refers to the full acceptance of the client by the coach, providing a safe space where the client can openly explore thoughts and feelings without judgment. The application of this principle can help build a trusting relationship and facilitate more open communication.

Exercise: The 'Best-Self' Visualization

Invite the client to engage in a guided visualization exercise where they imagine their 'best-self' operating in various facets of life. This not only serves as motivation but can also highlight specific areas where the client would like to improve.

Humanistic psychology also encourages addressing existential questions about meaning, purpose, and values. Coaches can use questionnaires or guided conversations to help clients explore these deeper layers of their existence, fostering a greater sense of personal alignment and meaning.

By incorporating the principles rooted in humanistic psychology, life coaches can offer a deeply personalized and empowering pathway for their clients, encouraging them not just to meet specific life goals but to seek a higher level of personal fulfillment and self-actualization.

CHAPTER 6

POPULAR MODELS IN COACHING

re you eager to dive into the foundational frameworks that life coaches across the globe rely on? Chapter 6, "Popular Models in Coaching," is tailored to introduce you to three seminal coaching models that have stood the test of time and proven their efficacy in multiple coaching environments.

From the client-centric CLEAR Model to the solution-oriented GROW Model and the results-driven OSCAR Model, this chapter will furnish you with the blueprints you need to navigate various coaching scenarios. You'll learn not just what these models are but how to deploy them seamlessly in your practice to guide your clients through self-discovery, goal setting, and effective action.

Here's what you can expect:

» CLEAR Model: Learn the essentials of this cutting-edge framework that stands for Contracting, Listening, Exploring, Action, and Review. Understand how to create a robust coaching agreement and guide the coaching conversation for maximum impact.

» GROW Model: Delve into this classic model that has been the backbone of life coaching. Master the four pillars—Goals, Reality, Options, and Will—to offer your clients a structured pathway to their aspirations.

» OSCAR Model: Acquaint yourself with this lesser-known but highly effective coaching model. Learn to guide your clients through Outcome, Situation, Choices, Actions, and Review to achieve measurable and meaningful results.

By the end of this chapter, you'll be armed with versatile techniques and structured models to facilitate impactful coaching sessions. Whether you're helping a client make a career transition, improve personal relationships, or work on self-improvement, these models offer a proven roadmap for success.

The CLEAR Model

The CLEAR Model is an increasingly popular framework within the coaching community, specifically designed to bring structure and effectiveness to the coaching process. The acronym CLEAR stands for Contracting, Listening, Exploring, Action, and Review. This model offers a multi-dimensional approach to life coaching, giving coaches the tools to foster deep engagement and transformative changes for their clients. Let's dive into each component.

Contracting

The first stage of the CLEAR model involves forming a contract or agreement with your client. This is more than just paperwork; it's an emotional and psychological commitment to a mutual journey. You need to establish parameters like:

» Duration and frequency of sessions
» Objectives of the coaching relationship

> » Boundaries and confidentiality
> » How progress will be measured and evaluated

Practical Tip: Begin your first session with a 'Contracting Discussion' where you lay out these terms clearly, asking your client for input and agreement. A shared Google Doc can work well for this.

Listening

Active listening is vital in coaching. In this stage, your primary role is to listen deeply, not just to the words your client uses, but also to their emotional cues, body language, and the unsaid.

Practical Tip: Practise "Reflective Listening" by repeating back what the client has said in your own words, asking for confirmation or clarification. This reinforces that you're engaged and also helps the client see their issues more clearly.

Exploring

Exploration is the heart of the coaching relationship. This is where you and your client delve into issues, challenges, and opportunities, looking for insights and solutions. Open-ended questions are your best tool here, allowing your client to do the thinking and learning.

Practical Tip: Utilize questions like "What do you think might be the root cause of this challenge?" or "How would your life change if you could resolve this issue?" to provoke deep thinking.

Action

Action is the turning point where talking turns into doing. You'll guide your client to form actionable steps to reach their goals, using SMART objectives for clarity and measurability.

Practical Tip: Use a shared action plan document where both you and the client can log objectives, strategies, and timelines. Update this after each session.

The CLEAR model isn't complete without a thorough review. This involves going over what has been achieved and what needs to be adjusted. Honest feedback is crucial here.

Practical Tip: Use the last 10 minutes of your session for a quick review or schedule periodic review sessions. Always ask for feedback, both positive and negative, to understand your client's perspective and continuously refine your approach.

Exercises for CLEAR Model Mastery

- » Contracting Exercise: Create a sample contracting document that you can customize for each new client.
- » Listening Exercise: Record a mock session and play it back, focusing only on your listening skills. Did you interrupt? Did you provide space for the client to think and respond?
- » Exploring Exercise: Develop a list of 20 powerful open-ended questions that you can use in various scenarios.
- » Action Exercise: Make a blank action plan template. Include sections for objectives, actions, deadlines, and a checkbox for when each action is complete.
- » Review Exercise: After each session, write down one thing that went well and one area where you could improve.

Arming yourself with the CLEAR model can immensely refine your approach and make your coaching sessions more focused, measurable, and, most importantly, impactful.

The GROW Model

The GROW Model is one of the most well-established and widely used coaching frameworks globally, helping coaches guide clients through a structured, yet flexible, process that fosters self-awareness and actionable insights. The acronym GROW stands for Goal, Reality, Options, and Will. In this detailed exploration of the GROW Model, we'll dissect each phase, offering you practical tips and exercises to implement in your coaching sessions.

Goal

The first stage, Goal, is where you help your client articulate what they want to achieve. This could be a short-term objective or a long-term aspiration. The focus here is clarity and specificity.

Practical Tip: Use questions like "What does success look like for you?" or "How will you know when you've achieved this goal?" to crystallize your client's objectives. Consider using visual aids like vision boards to make these goals more tangible.

Reality

Once the goal is set, the Reality stage invites clients to assess their current situation concerning their objectives. This involves identifying both the assets at their disposal and the challenges they face.

Practical Tip: Use a SWOT analysis (Strengths, Weaknesses, Opportunities, Threats) to provide a structured approach to examining the current reality. Ask questions like "What resources do you have?" and "What is stopping you?"

Options

The Options phase

This phase is about brainstorming. This is the stage where you help your client think broadly about the possible routes they could take to achieve their goals. Creativity is key here, and it's important to avoid immediately dismissing any ideas.

Practical Tip: Encourage your client to think outside the box by asking questions like "What would you do if you had unlimited resources?" or "Who could help you achieve this goal?" Also, consider using mind-mapping techniques to explore all possibilities visually.

Will

The Will stage is where the rubber meets the road. Your client needs to decide which options to pursue and commit to specific actions. This is also where you discuss obstacles and how to overcome them.

Practical Tip: Utilize SMART criteria to refine and quantify the action steps. Ensure that there's a timeline and a way to measure success. Create an "Action Commitment Sheet" that the client can take away from the session.

Exercises for GROW Model Mastery

> » Goal-Setting Exercise: Develop a set of probing questions designed to unearth your client's deepest aspirations.

> » Reality Check Exercise: Create a printable SWOT analysis template that clients can fill out during the session.

> » Options Exercise: Use a whiteboard or digital mind-mapping tool to brainstorm options in a free-form manner. This could be done as homework or during the session.

> » Willpower Exercise: Create a commitment contract for your client to sign, specifying the actions they will take before the next session.

By mastering the GROW Model, you'll be equipping yourself with a tried-and-true framework that can bring both structure and flexibility to your coaching sessions. This model offers a holistic view, covering all the bases from aspiration to action, making it an invaluable tool in your coaching arsenal.

SWOT Analysis Worksheet for Coaching Session

Client Name: ________________________ Date: ________________

Instructions:

Please consider your current situation in relation to your set goals and complete each quadrant with as much detail as possible. The aim is to identify your Strengths, Weaknesses, Opportunities, and Threats to better understand your reality and resources.

Strengths

What are your core skills?

What unique resources can you access?

What external assets exist that you can leverage?

Weaknesses

What areas need improvement?

What resources are you lacking?

What external challenges could hinder your progress?

Opportunities

What new avenues are opening up for you?

What external opportunities can you exploit?

What goals are now achievable?

Are there emerging trends you can take advantage of?

Threats

What internal obstacles do you face?

What external challenges could impede you?

Are any of your weaknesses becoming threats?

Are there unfavorable trends that you should be aware of?

Key Takeaways:

Strengths: ____

Weaknesses: ____

Opportunities: ____

Threats: ____

The OSCAR Model in Life Coaching

While the GROW model is popular in life coaching, the OSCAR model is another valuable framework that coaches can use to guide their clients effectively. The OSCAR Coaching Model offers a well-structured approach that begins with identifying clear outcomes and understanding the current situation. It then moves on to exploring various choices for action, subsequently focusing on actionable steps and, finally, conducting a review to measure results and make adjustments as necessary.

This cycle not only provides a clear direction but also encourages creative thinking and holds the client accountable for their own progress. Furthermore, its versatility allows it to be applied across different areas of life, making it an empowering tool for both coaches and clients.

OSCAR stands for Outcome, Situation, Choices, Actions, and Review.

Here's an overview of each component:

Outcome: Define What You Want to Achieve

» Objective: The first step is to establish the desired outcome. What is the client's end goal?

» Key Questions:

>> What do you want to achieve?

>> How will you know when you've achieved it?

» Exercise: Have the client write down their specific outcome in a single, clear sentence.

Situation: Assess the Current State

» Objective: Identify and understand the current reality. What is happening in the client's life right now?

» Key Questions:

  » What is the current situation?

  » What challenges are you facing?

» Exercise: Complete a SWOT analysis to understand strengths, weaknesses, opportunities, and threats relevant to the situation.

Choices: Explore Available Options

» Objective: Identify different choices available for moving from the current situation to the desired outcome.

» Key Questions:

  » What options do you have?

  » What else could you do?

» Exercise: Brainstorming session to list all possible choices. Encourage creative thinking and non-traditional solutions.

Actions: Plan and Commit

» Objective: Decide on a set of actions to take, to move closer to the outcome.

» Key Questions:

  » What will you do?

  » When will you do it?

» Exercise: Create an action plan detailing what steps need to be taken, assigning deadlines and responsibilities.

Review: Reflect and Adjust

» Objective: After the actions have been executed, it's essential to review and assess the effectiveness.

» Key Questions:

  » What worked well?

  » What could be improved?

» Exercise: Schedule a follow-up session for a review. Look at the action plan and compare it to actual results.

The OSCAR model provides a structured, step-by-step approach for tackling complex issues and it ensures that both coach and client remain focused on actionable outcomes. Regular reviews are crucial for understanding the effectiveness of the actions and for making necessary adjustments.

By acquainting yourself with the OSCAR model, you'll be better equipped to guide your clients through a structured process that will help them make measurable and meaningful progress toward their goals.

CHAPTER 7

COGNITIVE BEHAVIORAL COACHING

Cognitive Behavioral Coaching (CBC) is based on Cognitive Behavioral Therapy (CBT). We will delve into the fascinating world of Cognitive Behavioral Coaching (CBC), a powerful approach that marries the scientific rigor of Cognitive Behavioral Therapy (CBT) with the client-focused flexibility of coaching. Learn how to help your clients identify and challenge distorted thought patterns, gain self-awareness, and employ behavioral techniques to achieve meaningful change. This comprehensive guide equips you with a range of proven strategies, insightful case studies, and interactive exercises. You'll understand how to create a synergistic coach-client relationship that fosters both insight and action. From managing anxiety and stress to overcoming procrastination, CBC offers a versatile toolkit for tackling a multitude of challenges. Don't miss this opportunity to add a transformative coaching style to your repertoire, one that could be the key to unlocking your clients' true potential. By the end of this chapter, you'll have a comprehensive understanding of Cognitive Behavioral Coaching, complete with proven strategies, case studies, and interactive exercises. This methodological addition to your coaching toolkit can help you guide clients through a range of challenges, from managing anxiety and stress to overcoming procrastination. It's an opportunity to deepen your coaching practice and unlock your clients' true potential.

Cognitive Behavioral Coaching and Its Roots in Cognitive Behavioral Therapy

Rooted in the well-established principles of Cognitive Behavioral Therapy (CBT), CBC is a fusion of psychological theory and coaching techniques designed to empower individuals to achieve their personal and professional goals. While CBT is generally employed to treat mental health disorders like depression and anxiety, CBC takes these potent psychological principles and applies them in a coaching context.

Unlike therapeutic settings that aim to heal and manage symptoms, CBC focuses on the here and now, empowering clients to become self-sufficient in managing their thoughts, emotions, and behaviors to optimize success. It's a practical, solution-focused approach that accentuates cognitive awareness and behavioral change. With CBC, the coach collaborates with the client to identify distorted thinking patterns, challenge them, and adopt more adaptive beliefs and actions.

What is CBC?

Definition and Key Principles of Cognitive Behavioral Coaching

Cognitive Behavioral Coaching (CBC) is a goal-oriented, client-focused approach that combines the principles and techniques of Cognitive Behavioral Therapy (CBT) with the practical, problem-solving framework of coaching. Unlike traditional coaching methods that might primarily focus on motivation or goal-setting, CBC delves into the interplay between thoughts, emotions, and behaviors. The approach recognizes that our thought patterns can significantly influence our actions and feelings, sometimes in ways that are counterproductive or self-sabotaging.

Here are some key principles that underpin CBC:

- » **Cognitive Awareness**: CBC emphasizes the understanding of one's own thought processes. It encourages clients to become aware of their limiting beliefs or cognitive distortions that may hinder their ability to reach their goals.

- » **Behavioral Activation**: The coaching process involves identifying detrimental behaviors and replacing them with more productive ones. This often follows the cognitive awareness stage and aims to put new thinking into action.

- » **Solution-Focused**: While recognizing the importance of understanding one's thought patterns, CBC is primarily solution-focused. It looks for immediate actions that can improve a situation or bring a client closer to their objectives.

- » **Collaborative Approach**: In CBC, the coach and client work as a team. The coach facilitates the client's self-discovery and problem-solving but doesn't offer advice or solutions. Instead, the client is empowered to find their own solutions through guided inquiry.

- » **Adaptability**: One of the key strengths of CBC is its adaptability. It can be applied to various aspects of life, from career development to personal growth, and is suitable for a diverse client base.

> » **Structured Framework**: CBC uses a structured, session-by-session framework, which allows both the coach and client to monitor progress and make data-driven decisions.

The Relationship Between CBT and CBC

Cognitive Behavioral Therapy (CBT) and Cognitive Behavioral Coaching (CBC) are closely related, sharing foundational principles and techniques but differing in their objectives, scope, and application.

Both CBT and CBC are rooted in cognitive-behavioral psychology, which emphasizes the interconnectedness of thoughts, emotions, and behaviors. They both utilize the principle that changing one's thought patterns can lead to changes in feelings and actions. Techniques like cognitive reframing, thought identification, and behavioral activation are commonly used in both approaches.

CBT is primarily designed to treat mental health issues like anxiety, depression, and phobias. It often aims to bring a client from a state of dysfunction to a state of function. CBC, on the other hand, generally targets individuals who are functioning adequately but seek improvement in specific areas of life or work. It aims to move a person from a state of function to a state of optimal function or excellence.

CBT is usually a longer-term engagement and may involve digging deeply into past experiences or traumas to understand and alter current thought patterns. CBC tends to be more focused and shorter-term, dealing with specific current challenges or goals the client wants to address.

CBT is conducted by mental health professionals who are licensed to diagnose and treat mental illnesses. CBC is usually done by certified coaches who do not diagnose or treat mental conditions but rather focus on helping clients achieve specific personal or professional objectives.

While CBT is applied in a clinical setting, CBC is more versatile and can be implemented in a variety of environments including corporate settings, educational institutions, and one-on-one personal coaching scenarios. Understanding the relationship between CBT and CBC can help you tailor your coaching strategies effectively, borrowing valuable principles and techniques from CBT while maintaining the goal-oriented, client-focused nature that defines coaching.

Benefits of Using CBC as a Life Coach

As a life coach, incorporating Cognitive Behavioral Coaching (CBC) into your toolkit can offer numerous advantages. There are some compelling reasons why CBC can be particularly effective.

One of the standout benefits of CBC is its versatility. The approach can be applied to a myriad of life issues, from career development and decision-making to relationship issues and stress management. Whether a client wants to overcome procrastination, build self-confidence, or manage time more effectively, CBC's flexible framework is adaptable to meet a wide range of objectives. This makes it an excellent tool for coaches who deal with clients facing diverse challenges.

CBC draws its roots from Cognitive Behavioral Therapy, a psychological approach that is well-researched and empirically supported. This science-backed foundation lends credibility and efficacy to CBC. Clients and coaches alike can have confidence in the techniques being employed, knowing that they are grounded in psychological theory and have been tested for their effectiveness in bringing about positive behavioral change.

CBC's focus on thought patterns and belief systems empowers clients to take control of their own lives. By recognizing how their thoughts influence their emotions and actions, clients can begin to enact meaningful change from within. This internal locus of control can be incredibly empowering and lends itself to long-lasting transformation.

Unlike some coaching methods that might rely on abstract theories, CBC is highly practical. It provides actionable steps and strategies that clients can immediately apply to their lives. This action-oriented nature makes it easier to track progress, measure outcomes, and adjust coaching interventions as needed.

The evidence-based nature of CBC can make it appealing to clients who appreciate a more scientific, less woo-woo approach to personal development. This broadens your potential client base, particularly among those who might be skeptical of coaching methods that lack empirical support.

By integrating cognitive, emotional, and behavioral components, CBC offers a holistic approach to problem-solving and personal development. This allows coaches to address the multifaceted nature of human experience, thereby leading to more comprehensive and enduring solutions for clients.

Identifying and Challenging Distorted Thoughts

One of the pivotal aspects of Cognitive Behavioral Coaching (CBC) is the identification and subsequent challenging of distorted thoughts. These are cognitive patterns that often hold clients back, keeping them mired in negativity or inaction. These distorted thoughts—also known as cognitive distortions—can significantly impact emotions, behavior, and overall well-being. In this section, we delve into the types of distorted thoughts commonly encountered and provide practical strategies for challenging them. Mastering this skill not only equips you with a powerful coaching tool but also empowers your clients to break free from self-limiting beliefs, paving the way for positive change.

Common Cognitive Distortions

Understanding the types of distorted thoughts that commonly plague individuals is the first step in challenging and ultimately changing them. Here are some of the most prevalent cognitive distortions that you may encounter during your coaching sessions:

1. All-or-Nothing Thinking: This is a form of extreme thinking where situations are viewed in black-and-white terms. A minor setback can be seen as a catastrophic failure.

2. Overgeneralization: Here, one negative event is taken as a pattern of failure. For example, failing to secure a job interview may lead the client to think they'll never get a job.

3. Mental Filtering: This involves focusing exclusively on negative aspects of a situation, filtering out any positive elements. It's like seeing the world through a lens tinted with negativity.

4. Jumping to Conclusions: This occurs when individuals make assumptions without sufficient evidence. Two common subtypes are "mind-reading" (assuming what

others are thinking) and "fortune-telling" (predicting events will turn out badly).

5. Catastrophizing: This involves imagining the worst possible scenario and treating it as though it's inevitable.

6. Personalization: Here, the client takes responsibility for external events that they had no control over, adding an undue burden of guilt or shame.

7. Emotional Reasoning: This involves taking emotions as evidence for the truth. "I feel bad, so it must be bad."

8. Labeling: Assigning labels to oneself or others based on limited information. For example, "I failed a test; I'm a failure."

9. Magnification and Minimization: Overestimating the importance of negative events while underestimating the significance of positive events.

10. Should Statements: Harboring rigid rules and berating oneself or others for not following them, often using terms like "should," "ought," or "must."

Recognizing these common cognitive distortions is crucial for both the coach and the client. It allows you to challenge these distorted thoughts and replace them with more balanced and rational thoughts, a core component of CBC.

Techniques for Challenging These Distortions

Identifying cognitive distortions is just the first step; the real work lies in challenging and reframing these thoughts. As a life coach, your role is to guide clients through this process, providing them with practical techniques to shift their thinking patterns. Below are some effective methods you can employ:

1. Thought Records

One of the most structured ways to challenge distorted thinking is to keep a Thought Record. The client writes down the distorted thought, the situation where it occurred, the emotion it elicited, and then works on providing evidence for and against it. Finally, they come up with a balanced thought to replace the distorted one.

Thought Records are essentially a journaling exercise aimed at dissecting a distorted thought to examine its validity. It's a multi-step process that allows the client to pause and reflect on what is going through their mind.

» Step 1: Identify the Situation: Ask the client to write down the specific situation where the distorted thought occurred. This could be an event, an interaction, or even a memory.

» Step 2: Capture the Emotion: What emotion did this thought trigger? It could be anxiety, anger, sadness, etc. Have the client rate the intensity of this emotion on a scale of 1 to 10.

» Step 3: Note the Distorted Thought: What exactly is the thought that's bothering the client? Have them write it down verbatim.

» Step 4: Evidence For and Against: Ask the client to list evidence supporting this thought and evidence against it. This is crucial for weighing the thought's validity.

» Step 5: Balanced Thought: Finally, encourage the client to come up with a more balanced, rational thought based on the evidence. Have them rate the intensity of their emotion again after considering this balanced thought.

Thought Records can be a transformative exercise, providing tangible evidence of cognitive distortions and how to challenge them.

2. Socratic Questioning

Socratic questioning is a dialogue-driven technique where you, as a coach, ask your client a series of thought-provoking questions aimed at stimulating critical thinking and illuminating underlying beliefs. The objective is to help your clients discover the inherent flaws or inconsistencies in their distorted thoughts.

Questions can range from exploratory queries like, "How did you arrive at that conclusion?" to more targeted ones like, "Is this thought based on facts or assumptions?"

The power of Socratic questioning comes from the self-discovery it encourages. When clients find the answers themselves, the impact is usually far more significant than being told the same information.

3. Decatastrophizing

The technique of decatastrophizing is employed primarily for thoughts that involve "worst-case scenario" thinking. It's about challenging the perceived catastrophic outcome by examining its actual probability and potential impact. For thoughts involving catastrophizing, you could ask the client to play out the scenario in their head, examining the realistic outcomes and how bad they would genuinely be. Often, the fear of an event is far more debilitating than the event itself.

1. Step 1: Identify the Worst-Case Scenario: What is the dreadful outcome that the distorted thought predicts? Have the client spell it out.

2. Step 2: Assess Probability: How likely is this worst-case scenario? Is it a one-in-a-million chance or more probable?
3. Step 3: Realistic Outcomes: Discuss more probable, less catastrophic outcomes.
4. Step 4: Coping Strategies: Even if the worst were to happen, discuss coping strategies and resources that could be employed.

This method puts the 'catastrophe' in perspective, reducing its emotional charge and making it more manageable.

4. Behavioral Experiments

Sometimes, the best way to challenge a thought is to test its validity. Encourage the client to change their behavior based on the opposite of what the distorted thought is telling them and observe the outcomes. This technique is about moving from theory to action. The client takes a distorted thought and essentially puts it to the test in real life.

» Step 1: Identify the Thought: What is the distorted thought to be tested?
» Step 2: Design the Experiment: Create a situation where this thought can be examined. It should be safe and achievable.
» Step 3: Execute: With your support, the client then carries out the experiment.
» Step 4: Reflect: After the experiment, sit down with the client to discuss the outcomes. What did they learn? Was the distorted thought disproved or validated?

Behavioral experiments offer empirical evidence that can be immensely powerful in changing thought patterns.

Absolutely, let's delve into the next set of techniques.

5. Mindfulness and Present Moment Awareness

Mindfulness techniques are designed to bring the client's attention to the present moment, thereby interrupting the cycle of rumination and distorted thinking. The act of being present can, in itself, be a counter to cognitive distortions.

- » Step 1: Awareness: Encourage the client to become aware of their thoughts, feelings, and sensations in the present moment without judgment.
- » Step 2: Observation: Ask the client to observe these experiences as if they were a disinterested third party, merely collecting data.
- » Step 3: Non-Judgment: Reinforce the importance of not labeling these thoughts and sensations as 'good' or 'bad.'
- » Step 4: Return: Whenever the mind wanders, gently bring attention back to the present.

Mindfulness not only challenges the distorted thought in the moment but also equips the client with a skill that can be applied universally.

6. Positive Reattribution

This technique is geared towards reframing distorted thoughts by attributing positive or neutral causes to events instead of negative ones.

- » Step 1: Identify the Negative Attribution: What cause is the client attributing to the event?

» Step 2: Challenge the Attribution: Ask the client if there are other, more positive or neutral, reasons for this event happening.

» Step 3: Weigh the Evidence: Encourage the client to consider evidence for each attribution.

» Step 4: Choose a Balanced Attribution: The client selects a more balanced reason for the event, one that is supported by evidence.

Positive reattribution helps in breaking the habit of instantly adopting a negative viewpoint and encourages more balanced thinking.

7. Reality Testing

Reality testing is a process of verifying the truthfulness of a thought or belief, often through empirical evidence.

» Step 1: Capture the Thought: What is the distorted thought?

» Step 2: Gather Evidence: What evidence is there to support this thought? What evidence is against it?

» Step 3: Analyze: Weigh the evidence and judge its reliability and relevance.

» Step 4: Conclude: Based on the evidence, is the thought likely to be true, false, or somewhere in between?

Reality Testing is a straightforward method, but its effectiveness lies in its empiricism. It forces the client to confront their cognitive distortions with hard evidence.

8. Identifying Core Beliefs

Sometimes, distorted thoughts are the symptoms of deeper, more entrenched beliefs. Identifying these core beliefs can sometimes help in alleviating multiple cognitive distortions at once.

> » Step 1: Trace the Thought: Encourage the client to think about where this thought stems from. Are there recurring themes in their distorted thoughts?
> » Step 2: Identify Potential Core Belief: Ask the client what this thought says about them as a person. This often reveals a core belief.
> » Step 3: Challenge the Core Belief: Just like with individual thoughts, core beliefs can and should be challenged for their validity.
> » Step 4: Develop a New Belief: Assist the client in constructing a new, healthier core belief to replace the old one.

Understanding core beliefs can be a transformative exercise as it attacks the issue at the root, leading to broader changes in thought patterns and behaviors.

These techniques offer a rich toolkit for life coaches who are serious about helping their clients overcome cognitive distortions. With a thorough understanding of each, you can tailor your approach to suit the specific needs and challenges your clients face.

The Role of Self-Awareness

In Cognitive Behavioral Coaching (CBC), self-awareness is not just a supplementary skill; it is a cornerstone upon which the whole coaching journey rests. It acts as the critical lens through which clients can scrutinize their thoughts, feelings, and actions, allowing them to identify distortions and work towards healthier patterns of thinking and behaving.

Self-awareness can often be the key that unlocks change. When a client becomes truly aware of their cognitive distortions, they move from a state of unconscious incompetence—being unaware of their shortcomings—to a state of conscious incompetence, recognizing that a problem exists. This is the first crucial step towards improvement and growth.

Unpacking Self-Awareness

Thought Recognition: At the most basic level, self-awareness begins with recognizing one's thoughts. This recognition forms the basis for all subsequent cognitive challenges and reframes in the CBC process.

Emotional Intelligence: Self-awareness extends to understanding one's emotional reactions and how they are influenced by distorted thinking. Emotional intelligence and self-awareness go hand-in-hand in CBC, helping clients navigate their emotional world more effectively.

Behavioral Insights: True self-awareness also encompasses an understanding of one's behavior. Clients learn to identify which actions result from distorted thinking and how they can make different choices moving forward.

Practical Tools for Enhancing Self-Awareness

Reflective Journaling: Encourage your clients to keep a journal that records their daily thoughts, emotional states, and behavioral patterns. This practice creates a 'map' of cognitive processes over time and can be instrumental in identifying recurring issues and distortions.

Mindfulness Exercises: As mentioned earlier, mindfulness is a potent tool for enhancing self-awareness. Practices like focused breathing or body scans help individuals become aware of their thoughts and feelings without judgment.

Feedback Loops: Clients can also build self-awareness by seeking honest feedback from trusted individuals in their lives. Sometimes an outside perspective can shed light on blind spots that one may not be aware of.

Self-Assessment Questionnaires: Psychological tests and questionnaires can offer structured insights into personality traits, emotional intelligence, and even specific cognitive distortions, enriching the client's self-awareness.

The Transformative Power of Self-Awareness

The beauty of embedding self-awareness into CBC is that it doesn't just serve the immediate coaching goals; it equips clients with a lifelong skill that is universally applicable. From personal relationships to professional challenges, a heightened sense of self-awareness can be a game-changer.

In CBC, self-awareness is both the starting point and the ongoing process, continually refined and deepened throughout the coaching journey. It's not just about solving problems; it's about equipping your clients with the self-knowledge and tools to continuously evolve and adapt throughout their lives.

Self-awareness is the lens through which the complexities of the human mind can be viewed, understood, and ultimately, transformed. As a coach employing CBC methods, fostering this vital skill in your clients will be one of your most impactful contributions.

Tools for increasing self-awareness

Here are some widely recognized self-assessment questionnaires and tests that can be found on the internet and be employed to boost self-awareness:

1. Belbin Team Roles Assessment: Focuses on assessing an individual's preferred role in a team environment.
2. StrengthsFinder: Now often referred to as CliftonStrengths, this tool helps individuals discover their top talent themes to maximize their potential.
3. DISC Profile: A behavior assessment tool that focuses on four primary attributes: Dominance, Influence, Steadiness, and Conscientiousness.
4. Big Five Personality Test: Examines one's five major dimensions of personality: Openness, Conscientiousness, Extraversion, Agreeableness, and Neuroticism.
5. The 16 Personalities Test: Based on the Myers-Briggs framework and the Big Five, it gives more detailed personality type results.
6. Emotional Intelligence (EI) Test: A series of questions that aim to evaluate an individual's ability to perceive, control, and evaluate emotions.
7. Enneagram Personality Test: Identifies individuals as one of nine types, each of which has its unique set of characteristics, desires, fears, and motivations.
8. FIRO-B (Fundamental Interpersonal Relations Orientation-Behavior): This tool evaluates how individuals

behave toward others and how they expect others to act toward them.

9. TAT (Thematic Apperception Test): A projective psychological test that assesses a person's patterns of thought, attitudes, observational capacity, and emotional responses.

10. Self-Compassion Scale: Measures how individuals act towards themselves in times of difficulty.

11. Values in Action Inventory (VIA Survey): Identifies character strengths in individuals.

12. Career Assessment Inventories: Tools like the Strong Interest Inventory or the Holland Codes (RIASEC) can help individuals understand their career interests and preferences.

13. Learning Styles Inventory: Helps to determine how individuals prefer to learn, which can be critical for designing self-awareness or self-improvement interventions.

14. Kolb's Experiential Learning Style Inventory: Assesses where an individual falls within Kolb's four styles: converging, diverging, assimilating, or accommodating.

It's essential to note that while these tools provide valuable insights, they are not definitive. Everyone is unique, and the results from these tests should be used as a guide rather than a fixed label.

Behavioral Techniques

Behavioral techniques are vital tools in the Cognitive Behavioral Coaching (CBC) toolkit, and they offer practical ways to encourage behavior change in clients. These methods are geared towards helping individuals replace unhelpful behaviors with more beneficial ones, thereby aligning their actions with their core values and goals. Below are some examples of commonly used behavioral techniques in CBC, along with guidance on how to employ these strategies in a coaching context.

1. Behavioral Activation

What it is: This technique involves helping your client identify activities that are aligned with their values and interests and encouraging them to engage in these activities, particularly when they're prone to avoidance or procrastination.

How to Use: Create a list of activities that the client enjoys or wants to engage in. Plan a schedule to incorporate these activities into their week. Review the outcomes in follow-up sessions.

2. Exposure Technique

What it is: Exposure techniques are designed to help clients face their fears or anxieties in a controlled and incremental manner.

How to Use: Identify the fear or anxiety the client wishes to conquer. Develop a hierarchy of situations that gradually expose the client to the fear, starting with the least anxiety-inducing. Guide the client through these exposures, offering support and encouragement.

3. Role-playing

What it is: Role-playing enables clients to rehearse for real-life situations that they find challenging. It's a safe space to practice communication, decision-making, or other interpersonal skills.

How to Use: Identify the situation the client needs help with. Act out the scenario during your coaching session, taking turns playing different roles. Provide feedback and adjust the approach as needed.

4. Self-Monitoring

What it is: Self-monitoring involves keeping a detailed log of specific behaviors to understand triggers, emotions, or situations that influence them.

How to Use: Encourage your client to keep a journal or use a tracking app to record instances of the behavior you're both working to change. Use this data for discussion and strategy development in your coaching sessions.

5. Reward Systems

What it is: This involves setting up a system of small rewards for achieving behavioral milestones. Positive reinforcement can significantly encourage behavior change.

How to Use: Work with your client to establish clear behavioral milestones and corresponding rewards. It could be as simple as taking a short break after an hour of work or buying something nice after a week of achieving set goals.

Time Management Techniques

What it is: These are a set of techniques aimed at helping clients use their time more effectively to achieve their goals. Methods could include to-do lists, the Eisenhower Box, or the Pomodoro Technique.

How to Use: Introduce various time management techniques to your client, then help them tailor a time management system that aligns with their lifestyle and goals.

By incorporating these behavioral techniques into your coaching approach, you offer your clients actionable ways to effect lasting change. It's crucial to remember that each client is different, and therefore, it may be necessary to tailor these techniques to suit individual needs and contexts.

Synergistic Coach-Client Relationship

In the realm of Cognitive Behavioral Coaching, the relationship between the coach and the client transcends mere interaction; it evolves into a synergistic partnership founded on trust and mutual respect. This relationship is not just instrumental for creating a safe space where the client feels valued and understood but also serves as the crucible for both insight and action.

In traditional coaching settings, the focus may predominantly be on goal-setting and attainment. However, CBC brings a unique dimension into this dynamic by also integrating psychological insights. The coach does not merely serve as an accountability partner but takes on a more nuanced role, catalyzing not just behavioral change but also fostering a deeper self-awareness in the client. This twofold approach is what sets CBC apart, and the quality of the coach-client relationship is integral to its success.

This relationship becomes a collaborative journey where both parties are invested in the client's personal and emotional growth. A good CBC coach knows how to balance being empathetic with being objective. This delicate equilibrium allows the client to explore their thoughts, feelings, and behaviors openly while also receiving constructive feedback that triggers actionable insights.

In this strong relational framework, the coach employs various CBC techniques to challenge cognitive distortions, offer alternative perspectives, and establish a pathway for achievable goals. This is where the richness of the relationship truly shines— each session becomes an opportunity for not just goal-oriented action but also meaningful personal discovery.

Therefore, when you, as a coach, foster this kind of relationship with your client, you create a unique ecosystem where psychological insight and proactive behavior coalesce into a comprehensive strategy for life improvement. And in such a nurturing environment, not only do barriers break down, but new possibilities also start to take form. It's a transformative experience that benefits both the coach and the client, each learning and growing through the shared journey.

The influence of a synergistic coach-client relationship extends far beyond the coaching sessions themselves. Clients often find that the trust and mutual respect cultivated within this partnership spill over into other areas of their lives. Improved interpersonal relationships, increased confidence in decision-making, and a stronger sense of self are just some of the ancillary benefits clients may experience. Similarly, coaches find the relationship enriching, as they gain deeper insights into human behavior and thought processes, honing their skills further with each session.

The continuity of the relationship also matters. It's not just about what happens within the confines of a scheduled meeting but about the ongoing dialogue and reflection that continues afterward. This continuous engagement solidifies the action plans and reinforces the insights gained, thereby making the coaching relationship a living, evolving entity that constantly adapts and grows.

Moreover, the bond between coach and client often serves as a form of accountability that is uniquely motivating. When clients genuinely believe that their coach is invested in their success, they are more inclined to take action and less likely to let obstacles deter them. At the same time, coaches are more able to fine-tune their approaches, drawing from the pool of trust and openness that the relationship affords.

It's crucial to recognize that this type of relationship doesn't happen by accident. It is built consciously, with both parties investing effort into nurturing it. For coaches, this means ongoing professional development, honing not just their CBC techniques but also their skills in empathy, active listening, and ethical integrity.

The synergistic coach-client relationship in the context of Cognitive Behavioral Coaching is a lynchpin for effective change. It's a two-way street that requires investment, intention, and immense respect. And the dividends it pays are invaluable—deep, transformative changes that empower both the coach and the client to reach new heights in their personal and professional lives.

Case Studies and Interactive Exercises in CBC

Case Study 1: Overcoming Procrastination

Situation: Sarah, a 35-year-old writer, was struggling with procrastination. She had deadlines looming but couldn't bring herself to start her work.

Approach: The coach employed CBC to challenge Sarah's distorted thoughts that contributed to her procrastination. The thought "It needs to be perfect" was identified and rephrased to "It needs to be done; perfection can come later."

Result: Sarah managed to meet her deadlines and reported feeling less anxiety about her work.

Case Study 2: Dealing with Social Anxiety

Situation: Mark, a college student, had debilitating social anxiety that affected his performance in group activities and presentations.

Approach: Using CBC, the coach helped Mark identify his catastrophizing thoughts like "I will embarrass myself" and replaced them with more rational thoughts like "I can handle this."

Result: Mark began participating more in group activities and managed to deliver a successful presentation.

Case Study 3: Navigating a Career Change

Situation: Emily, a 42-year-old marketing executive, was considering a drastic career change but was paralyzed by the fear of the unknown and financial instability.

Approach: Through a series of coaching sessions, Emily's coach applied Cognitive Behavioral Coaching techniques to dig deeper into the thoughts fueling her fears. They discovered Emily was anchored to a belief system that equated her self-worth to her job title and salary. By systematically dissecting these beliefs, the coach helped her understand that her worth wasn't solely defined by her career. Together, they developed more rational, evidence-based thoughts, such as "Changing careers is an opportunity for growth," and "Financial adjustments are manageable obstacles, not dead-ends."

Result: With renewed clarity and confidence, Emily transitioned into a role in non-profit management, a field she had always been passionate about, and reported increased job satisfaction and overall well-being.

Case Study 4: Improving Personal Relationships

Situation: Carlos, a 31-year-old software developer, found that he was increasingly isolated from his friends and family. He attributed this to his work schedule, but deep down, he was also afraid of opening up emotionally.

Approach: In employing CBC, the coach worked closely with Carlos to explore the cognitive distortions affecting his relationships. They identified a 'black-and-white' thinking pattern where Carlos thought he'd either be "completely understood or entirely rejected" by his loved ones. Through targeted discussions, they reframed these beliefs into more nuanced, realistic thoughts, like "It's okay to be vulnerable; not everyone has to understand me fully for me to have meaningful relationships." The coach also guided him through some behavioral experiments, like setting up a weekly catch-up with friends and calling his family more often, to challenge his fears and distorted thoughts in real-world settings.

Result: Carlos found himself enjoying a much richer, more rewarding social life, and felt closer to his friends and family than he had in years.

Both Emily and Carlos' stories serve as rich examples of how versatile and impactful Cognitive Behavioral Coaching can be in diverse life scenarios. Through CBC, both clients not only achieved their initial goals but also gained a deeper understanding of themselves and the cognitive processes that had been holding them back.

Interactive Exercise 1: Thought Record Exercise for Career Fears

Objective: To help clients identify and challenge irrational fears related to career changes or advancements.

Description: In this exercise, the client will use a Thought Record Sheet to document real-time thoughts and feelings when faced with career-related decisions or challenges. Over the course of a week, clients will write down specific situations where they felt anxious or fearful about their careers, the thoughts that raced through their minds during those situations, and the emotions they experienced.

Instructions:

1. First, provide the client with a Thought Record Sheet that has columns for 'Situation,' 'Thoughts,' and 'Emotions.'
2. Whenever the client is faced with a career-related fear or decision, instruct them to fill out the sheet immediately afterward, capturing the situation, the thought, and the emotion as specifically as possible.
3. During the next coaching session, review the Thought Record Sheet together. Analyze each entry to identify any patterns or recurring cognitive distortions.
4. Guide the client through re-framing these irrational thoughts into more balanced and rational thoughts.

Interactive Exercise 2: Behavioral Experiment for Social Anxiety

Objective: To challenge and change the distorted thoughts that contribute to social anxiety and isolation.

Description: The client will design a simple behavioral experiment to test the validity of a specific fear or assumption that keeps them from engaging socially. For example, they might fear that people will judge them if they go to a social event alone.

Instructions:

1. Discuss with the client to identify a specific fear or belief that is affecting their social life.
2. Together, formulate a behavioral experiment to test this belief. For instance, if the client believes they can't go to a social event alone, the experiment might be to attend a casual gathering by themselves and to observe people's reactions.
3. Before executing the experiment, ask the client to predict the outcome. Make sure to document this.
4. Once the experiment is done, have the client record the actual outcome, noting any differences between their prediction and what actually happened.
5. Review the results in your next session. Did the outcome support or challenge the client's initial belief? Use this real-world evidence to help the client reframe their distorted thoughts and beliefs, making them more congruent with reality.

Both exercises are designed to be practical applications of Cognitive Behavioral Coaching principles, aimed at offering clients both insight and action in overcoming their challenges.

PART III

CORE COACHING SKILLS AND TECHNIQUES

This part serves as the practical cornerstone of the book, designed to arm aspiring and existing life coaches with the essential skills and tools needed for effective coaching. This section will dive into the art and science of coaching methodologies, honing in on crucial competencies like active listening, questioning techniques, goal-setting strategies, and ethical considerations in the coaching relationship.

The aim is to transition from understanding the theoretical frameworks of coaching discussed in the earlier parts to being able to apply these principles in real-world coaching scenarios. Whether you're just starting out or are looking to refine your coaching techniques, this section promises a wealth of insights to make you more adept and confident in helping clients transform their lives.

CHAPTER 8

MASTERING THE ART OF QUESTIONING

The art of questioning is a cornerstone in the edifice of life coaching. It's not just about asking what comes to mind but knowing how to pose questions that act as keys to hidden compartments of the human psyche. In a coaching relationship, questions are more than a means to elicit information; they are a conduit for empowerment, a catalyst for introspection, and a framework for progress. When thoughtfully employed, questioning techniques can help to unpeel layers of complexity, making way for clarity and actionable solutions. By honing your questioning skills, you're not just becoming a better interrogator; you're transforming into a better coach—someone who can guide clients through the maze of their minds toward meaningful destinations. This chapter will serve as a comprehensive guide to mastering the art of questioning, an indispensable skill set that every life coach needs in their toolkit.

The Power of Questions

If words are the currency of coaching, then questions are the gold bullion. Questions possess immense power to affect change, to inspire, to heal, and to lead people toward their chosen paths. In the realm of life coaching, questions are not merely a device to prompt conversation; they are a mechanism for evoking awareness and inspiring action.

When crafted and timed well, a single question can act as a pivot around which the client's perception can swing from confusion to clarity, or from procrastination to action. It can unearth buried emotions, triggering a cascade of realizations that might otherwise have remained inaccessible. Questions can be mirrors reflecting the client's inner world, magnifiers that reveal intricate details, or windows that open new vistas. They can serve as the nudge that topples the first domino, setting off a chain reaction of positive change.

In the hands of a skillful coach, questions can become instruments of transformation. They can push boundaries, challenge the status quo, and offer new paradigms. They can liberate clients from the shackles of limiting beliefs and empower them with the confidence to pursue their dreams. A well-placed question can be the spark that lights the fire of change, making it one of the most potent tools in a life coach's arsenal.

By understanding and harnessing the power of questions, you can facilitate profound shifts in your clients, guiding them not just toward external goals, but also toward a deeper understanding of themselves. This is the true essence of coaching: not to provide answers, but to facilitate the discovery of answers that are already within the client, waiting to be revealed.

Types of Questions

1. Open-Ended Questions: These are your best friends in a coaching session. Learn the skill of phrasing questions that require more than just a 'yes' or 'no' answer, provoking deeper thinking and self-examination.
2. Closed-Ended Questions: While not as explorative, closed-ended questions have their place, especially when you need to clarify information or make a decision quickly.
3. Reflective Questions: These questions mirror what the client has said, offering them a chance to explore their thoughts and feelings further.
4. Hypothetical Questions: These questions encourage clients to explore scenarios that haven't occurred yet, aiding them in understanding their feelings, attitudes, and reactions toward possible future events.

The Socratic Method

The Socratic Method is an ancient but ever-relevant art of questioning that coaches can adapt to facilitate deeper understanding and problem-solving. It involves asking a series of questions to stimulate critical thinking and illuminate ideas.

It's equally important to know what not to ask. Avoid leading questions, multiple questions, and questions that may imply judgment.

Exercises for Enhancing Your Questioning Skills

1. Questioning Journal: Maintain a journal to jot down impactful questions that come to mind during sessions or at any other time. Review these regularly to refine your questioning skills.

2. Role-play: Engage in mock coaching sessions with a peer. Take turns playing both the coach and client, focusing specifically on the questions being asked.

CHAPTER 9

BUILDING RAPPORT AND TRUST

In the dance of life coaching, rapport and trust are the music that guides the steps. Without them, the relationship between the coach and client is reduced to mere transactional exchanges, lacking the depth and emotional resonance necessary for transformative work. Yet, establishing trust and rapport isn't an accidental occurrence; it's a deliberate act that requires attentiveness, skill, and sincerity. In this chapter, we delve into the art and science of building a trustworthy and harmonious coaching relationship. We'll explore techniques like affirmations, confidentiality assurances, and the role of empathy, all aimed at cementing a foundation of mutual trust and respect.

Trust is not just a feeling; it's a critical framework that dictates how vulnerable a client is willing to be. It's the safety net that encourages risk-taking, the glue that holds the coaching relationship together. When trust is in the equation, clients are more likely to be open about their fears, dreams, and challenges, enabling the coach to provide more impactful guidance. Trust enhances the depth of the conversations and enriches the quality of the coaching experience.

Techniques for Building Trust

Affirmations

Using affirmations is not just a way to boost your client's self-esteem but also a powerful tool to affirm the safe space you're creating together. Affirmations like "I believe in you," or "You're capable of achieving your goals," can instill a sense of confidence in your client that further elevates the level of trust.

Confidentiality Assurances

Openness is the lifeblood of coaching, and it flourishes only when the client is assured of confidentiality. Make it a point to explicitly discuss your commitment to confidentiality, perhaps even integrating it into your coaching agreement, to make your client feel secure.

Empathy

Showing empathy goes beyond mere understanding; it's about sharing the emotional space your client occupies, without judgment. Empathetic coaching amplifies trust as clients feel seen, heard, and understood on a deeply emotional level.

Maintaining Rapport

Trust and rapport, once established, need ongoing nourishment. A lapse in either can significantly derail the coaching process.

Checking in on Past Actions

Regular check-ins serve as gentle accountability nudges. They remind the client of their commitments and show that you are invested in their progress. This not only maintains but often strengthens rapport.

Celebrating Small Wins

Don't wait for the end goal to celebrate; acknowledge and appreciate the small wins along the way. Whether it's a newfound insight, a conquered fear, or a tiny step toward a larger goal, celebrating these victories creates a positive loop of trust and rapport.

Rapport and trust are not one-time achievements; they're dynamic aspects of the coaching relationship that need constant attention. Utilizing techniques like affirmations, confidentiality assurances, and empathy can go a long way in building a robust and effective coaching environment. Keeping the momentum through regular check-ins and celebrating even the smallest progress ensures that the relationship stays as vibrant and productive as it started. After all, in the arena of life coaching, trust is both the starting line and the finish line, encompassing everything that happens in between.

CHAPTER 10

GOAL SETTING AND ACTION PLANNING

In this pivotal chapter, we turn our focus to one of the cornerstones of effective coaching: goal-setting and monitoring. The practice of setting goals is far more nuanced than simply identifying what the client wishes to achieve. It's an intricate interplay of understanding one's deepest desires, aligning them with actionable steps, and creating a system of accountability. In this space, the role of a life coach transcends that of a mere advisor to become a collaborator in the client's journey toward self-improvement and fulfillment.

We will explore various methods and frameworks for setting smart, achievable goals, touching on both popular and lesser-known techniques. The chapter will also delve into the art of goal monitoring—how to keep your client on track without being intrusive, how to adapt plans that are not working, and how to celebrate the milestones along the way.

In essence, this chapter aims to equip you with the tools, knowledge, and confidence to help your clients not just set but achieve their most cherished goals. Whether you're a new coach starting out or an experienced professional looking to refresh your skills, this chapter promises to add valuable insights to your coaching toolbox.

The Importance of Goal-Setting

The psychological basis for setting goals is deeply rooted in human nature. Our minds are hardwired to seek purpose and direction, and setting goals provides that critical framework for our ambitions and endeavors. Goal-setting not only motivates us to take action but also serves as a guiding star that focuses our energies towards a specific outcome. It gives us a sense of direction and purpose, making our journeys, whether personal or professional, more meaningful and impactful.

By setting goals, you give your client the roadmap they need to navigate the complexities of life's challenges. The act of articulating a goal transforms a vague wish into a concrete objective, turning abstract concepts into measurable outcomes. It becomes easier to formulate strategies, allocate resources, and determine what skills and tools are necessary for success. Ultimately, goal-setting creates an enabling structure that makes daunting tasks seem more manageable, breaking down complex objectives into smaller, achievable steps.

Examples of the Transformative Power of Well-Set Goals

1. The Career Changer: Consider the case of Sarah, a client who came to a life coach with a burning desire to switch careers. She was in corporate finance but longed to be a teacher. Her coach helped her set detailed and achievable goals, starting with taking weekend courses on educational

theory to volunteering at a local school. Within a year, Sarah was able to transition fully into her new role as a high school math teacher. Her well-set goals provided a clear path through a maze of uncertainty and doubt.

2. The Aspiring Athlete: Then there's David, a young man with aspirations of becoming a professional soccer player but struggling with confidence issues. With the help of his coach, he set progressive goals, beginning with improving specific skills, then moving to join a local team, and eventually aiming for scouting events. Each accomplished goal not only improved his skills but also built his confidence. A few years down the line, David received a scholarship for a university where he could play soccer at a competitive level.

3. The Wellness Seeker: Emily had struggled with weight and health issues for years. Her life coach helped her set realistic health goals, beginning with daily walks and graduating to more complex workout routines. They also worked on nutrition plans and stress management techniques. Today, Emily has lost over 50 pounds and run her first half-marathon.

These stories underline how the process of thoughtful goal-setting can transform lives in significant ways, setting individuals on paths they once only dreamed of walking. The key lies in the simple yet profound act of specifying what one wants to achieve and then creating a structured plan to make it happen.

Frameworks for Goal-Setting

When it comes to translating aspirations into concrete plans, the structure is crucial. While it's empowering to dream big, the journey from where you are to where you want to go must be mapped out meticulously. This is where goal-setting frameworks come in, providing a structured methodology to ensure that goals are not just inspiring but also attainable, measurable, and aligned with broader life objectives.

One of the most popular and widely recognized frameworks for goal-setting is the S.M.A.R.T model. This acronym stands for Specific, Measurable, Achievable, Relevant, and Time-bound. The S.M.A.R.T approach insists that a goal should be as specific as possible and that you should be able to measure progress towards its achievement. It should be realistic, meaning it's achievable with the available resources and in the existing constraints. The goal should also be relevant to larger life or career aims, and it must have a time-frame within which it will be achieved.

Another noteworthy framework is the CLEAR model, which places a more significant emphasis on the emotional and relational aspects of achieving objectives. CLEAR stands for Collaborative, Limited, Emotional, Appreciable, and Refinable. Collaborative goals encourage teamwork and make individual goals more sustainable and enjoyable. Limited goals are constrained by resources and time, much like the S.M.A.R.T model. Emotional goals tap into your intrinsic motivation, thereby increasing commitment. Appreciable goals can be broken down into smaller tasks, making them less overwhelming. Lastly, Refinable goals are flexible and can be adjusted as circumstances change, allowing for agility in approach.

There are various other frameworks like OKR (Objectives and Key Results), which is popular in the corporate world for setting ambitious goals and tying them to measurable results, or the WOOP model (Wish, Outcome, Obstacle, Plan), which encourages you to visualize the end result but also to foresee possible obstacles in your path.

Choosing the right framework depends on your client's specific needs, their emotional state, the nature of the goal, and the resources at hand. Each framework offers a different lens through which to view the goal-setting process, and savvy coaches can even blend elements from different frameworks to create a custom-tailored approach that best suits their client's situation.

The Coach's Role in Goal-Setting

Goal-setting is not just a client's endeavor; it's a collaborative process where the coach plays a pivotal role. One of the most essential skills in this context is active listening. While clients often come with a set of goals they want to achieve, it's not uncommon for these to be surface-level objectives. By employing active listening, a coach can delve deeper into the client's true aspirations, sometimes unearthing goals that even the client wasn't fully aware of. This process may involve probing questions, reflective listening, and paraphrasing to ensure that what is being said is mutually understood.

Active listening is not just about understanding the words but grasping the emotional subtext and the hidden motivations behind them. By doing so, a coach can guide the client to articulate goals that are not just desirable but deeply meaningful. These meaningful goals are often the ones that have the intrinsic power to motivate and inspire sustained action.

However, while it's important to aim high, it's equally crucial not to set the bar too high too quickly. This is where the coach's role in challenging the client comes in. A good coach knows how to stretch the client's capabilities without snapping their willpower or motivation. Achievable yet stretching goals create a sweet spot, providing both a challenge and a realistic path to success.

For instance, if a client aims to lose weight, setting a goal to lose 50 pounds in a month is not just unrealistic but also unhealthy. On the flip side, aiming to lose one pound a month might not provide enough of a challenge to incite meaningful change. Here, the coach's expertise and questioning techniques can help recalibrate these objectives to something like losing 5 to 8 pounds a month, making it both challenging and achievable.

In essence, the coach's role in goal-setting is that of a catalyst and a reality-checker, someone who helps the client articulate what they truly want to achieve and then steers them toward a plan that makes those dreams attainable. This balance between aspiration and practicality is what transforms the coaching relationship into a powerful engine for life-changing progress.

Techniques to facilitate effective brainstorming sessions

The process of goal-setting often starts with brainstorming, an invaluable method to liberate creativity and open up a myriad of possibilities. As a coach, facilitating effective brainstorming sessions can set the stage for the development of highly impactful goals. Here's how to do it.

Begin by creating a non-judgmental space. It's essential for the client to feel free to share any idea, no matter how outlandish it might initially seem. Reiterate the purpose of brainstorming, which is to generate a variety of options, not to evaluate them. Make it clear that the more ideas brought to the table, the better, as this widens the scope of possibilities and could lead to discovering hidden gems.

Secondly, deploy the power of open-ended questions. While it's tempting to jump in with suggestions or fill any awkward silences, resist that urge. Questions like, "What would you do if money were not a concern?" or "What activities make you lose track of time?" can elicit responses that might not surface otherwise. Your role is to guide the discussion rather than direct it.

Thirdly, consider using mind-mapping or other visual aids. Some people find it easier to express their thoughts visually rather than verbally. A diagram or a simple drawing can serve as a focus point, helping to structure the brainstorming session and making connections between different ideas more apparent.

Then there's the technique of role reversal. This involves asking the client to step into the shoes of someone they admire or someone who has already achieved what they aspire to. Questions like, "What would [Person X] do in this situation?" can provide fresh perspectives and inspire novel solutions.

Lastly, keep the energy up but also know when to wrap it up. An effective brainstorming session is often energetic and free-flowing, but it should also be time-bound. Once you have gathered an ample number of ideas, guide the client toward categorizing them, exploring their potential impact, and ultimately selecting those that resonate the most for further development.

By incorporating these techniques into your coaching sessions, you can make the brainstorming process not just productive but also deeply engaging. This not only leads to better goal-setting but also strengthens the rapport between you and your client, reinforcing the collaborative nature of the coaching relationship.

The Importance of Celebrating Milestones

One of the most overlooked yet critical elements in the goal-setting and achievement process is the act of celebrating milestones. While our eyes are often set on the finish line, we must not forget that the journey to that ultimate goal is fraught with ups and downs, challenges and triumphs. Recognizing and celebrating these milestones, however small, have profound psychological and motivational benefits that cannot be understated.

Psychological Benefits of Celebrating Small Wins

Psychologically, celebrating small victories creates a sense of accomplishment and significance. It's human nature to enjoy recognition and affirmation. Small wins act as checkpoints that offer us the emotional sustenance to continue the journey. Such celebrations produce dopamine, the 'feel-good' neurotransmitter, thereby boosting our mood and morale. They remind us that we are making progress, however incremental, towards something meaningful. This can be incredibly reaffirming for individuals who may be feeling stuck or discouraged.

Techniques to Mark Milestones

Various techniques can be used to mark milestones, ranging from simple verbal affirmations to more elaborate rewards. These can include:

1. Goal Boards: Using a physical or digital goal board where milestones can be marked and visually represented.
2. Achievement Journal: Keeping a dedicated journal where every small win, every milestone reached, is recorded. The act of writing itself can be therapeutic and validating.
3. Scheduled Reviews: Holding specific sessions dedicated to reviewing and acknowledging progress. Here, you can employ visual aids like charts or graphs to make the progress palpable.
4. Reward System: Creating a tiered system of rewards that correspond to different milestones can be highly motivating. These rewards can be material or experiential, depending on what resonates most with your client.
5. Public Recognition: If appropriate and with the client's consent, milestones can be celebrated in a more public forum, such as social media or a community group. Public affirmation can often amplify the sense of achievement.

How Celebrations Can Further Motivate and Inspire Clients

The act of celebrating milestones goes beyond immediate psychological gratification. It serves as a wellspring for future motivation. Each milestone reached and celebrated reinforces the client's self-belief and capacity to achieve. It serves as both a reminder of what has been accomplished and an inspiration for what can be achieved going forward. The positive energy generated from a celebration can be harnessed to tackle the next phase with renewed vigor and enthusiasm. Moreover, it sets a positive precedent, not just for the individual client but also for the coaching relationship. It cements trust, fosters a deeper emotional connection, and essentially lays the foundation for a more productive and mutually rewarding engagement.

Celebrating milestones, therefore, is not a mere act of indulgence but a strategic tool that can significantly influence the effectiveness of the coaching process. It enforces a sense of purpose, fortifies mental resilience, and continually fuels the motivation needed to achieve those larger life goals.

PART IV

ADVANCED COACHING

STRATEGIES

D ive into the next frontier of life coaching with Part IV: Advanced Coaching Strategies. Whether you're navigating the complexities of client resistance or orchestrating transformative group sessions, this section is your roadmap to mastery. Learn scientifically-backed techniques to help your clients regulate their emotions and innovative methods to break through resistance. Fine-tune your skills for the multi-faceted world of group coaching, both in-person and online. This part promises to equip you with tools and insights that will set you apart in your coaching journey. Ready to elevate your practice? The next level awaits.

CHAPTER 11

TECHNIQUES FOR OVERCOMING RESISTANCE

Resistance is a natural part of any transformative process. Even the most committed clients may harbor unconscious barriers or express overt reluctance that can impede progress. The challenge for life coaches is not to eliminate resistance, but to navigate it in a way that fosters deeper understanding and encourages constructive change. This chapter delves into advanced techniques for identifying and overcoming resistance, using methods like reframing, paradoxical intention, and positive confrontation.

The Nature of Resistance

Before delving into how to tackle resistance, it's crucial to understand its various forms. Resistance can manifest as skepticism, procrastination, defensiveness, or even overt refusal to participate in exercises or discussions. Understanding the type and source of resistance is the first step in addressing it effectively.

Reframing Resistance

Reframing involves changing the perspective or context within which a situation is viewed. When a client is resistant, reframing can help them see the obstacle not as a stopping point, but as an opportunity for greater insight. For example, if a client says, "I can't do this," you might reframe it by asking, "What's making this difficult for you?"

Reframing is one of the most powerful tools in a coach's arsenal for navigating resistance. The idea behind reframing is not to change the reality of the situation but to alter the lens through which it's viewed. Resistance often stems from preconceived notions or limiting beliefs that a client holds. By reframing these thoughts, coaches can guide clients toward a perspective that may be more beneficial or constructive for them.

Reframing works well because it sidesteps direct confrontation with the client's resistance, instead inviting them to consider an alternative viewpoint. People are naturally more willing to change their minds when they feel they've arrived at a new conclusion themselves, rather than being told they're wrong. Reframing offers an invitation to explore, rather than a mandate to change.

Techniques for Reframing

1. Labeling: Sometimes, resistance comes from how a situation or task is labeled. By simply changing the language around it, you can alleviate some of the resistance. For instance, instead of "workout," some might prefer the term "physical activity."

2. Perspective Shift: Ask your clients how a trusted friend or mentor might view their situation. This can help them step

out of their current mindset and consider alternative perspectives.

3. Scaling: If a client is feeling overwhelmed by a problem, ask them to scale the severity of the issue from 1 to 10. Then ask, "What would it take to move it down just one notch?" This breaks down a large problem into smaller, more manageable tasks.

4. The 'What If' Game: Encourage clients to explore alternative scenarios. What if the very thing they're resisting holds the key to something they've always wanted? What would that look like?

Examples

1. Client with Career Anxiety: Imagine a client who is extremely anxious about asking for a promotion. They might say something like, "I can't ask for a promotion; what if they say no?" A reframe could be, "What opportunities for growth could a 'no' provide you?"

2. Client Avoiding a Difficult Conversation: A client might say, "I can't talk to my spouse about our financial troubles. It'll just start a fight." A reframe could be, "How might that difficult conversation be the first step toward a solution you both need?"

By shifting the focus from limitations to possibilities, reframing opens up a space for the client to move past their resistance. It's like mental alchemy, turning obstacles into opportunities. Mastering this technique can greatly enhance your effectiveness as a life coach, helping you guide your clients through their resistance to a place of greater openness and receptivity.

Paradoxical Intention

This is a psychological technique wherein you instruct the client to intentionally think or behave in a manner opposite to their resistance. The goal is to make the client more aware of their barriers by exaggerating them. For instance, if a client is procrastinating, you might ask them to intentionally procrastinate more, but to also note down their feelings and thoughts during this period.

Paradoxical intention is a fascinating and counterintuitive strategy often used to deal with resistance. Rooted in the work of Viktor Frankl, a psychiatrist and the founder of logotherapy, this technique involves encouraging clients to deliberately think or behave in line with their fears or undesired traits. The irony is that by intentionally engaging with the very issue they're resisting, clients often find the issue loses its power over them.

This technique operates on the principle of paradox: when you stop trying to resist a certain behavior or thought pattern, it often diminishes in intensity or disappears. The reason paradoxical intention is so effective is that it helps to remove the added stress and anxiety that comes from resisting a particular thought or behavior, thereby reducing its impact.

How to Apply Paradoxical Intention

1. Identify the Resistance: First, pinpoint the specific thought, behavior, or emotion the client is resisting.
2. Propose the Paradox: Encourage the client to engage intentionally in the behavior or thought they are resisting. This could be as simple as saying, "Okay, let's assume the worst-case scenario does happen. What then?"

3. Reflect: After the exercise, ask the client to reflect on their experience. Often, they'll find that the act of willingly engaging with their fear reduced its intensity.

4. Review and Refine: Use the reflections as material for further coaching, either to deepen the work around the resistance or to move on to other areas now that the resistance has lessened.

Examples in Practice

1. Fear of Failure: If a client is paralyzed by the fear of failing a project, you might encourage them to spend a few minutes visualizing the worst-case outcome. What would life be like if they did fail? Often, this makes the client realize that failure isn't the end of the world, thus reducing the fear's hold on them.

2. Social Anxiety: For someone afraid of social interactions, encourage them to intentionally make what they fear would be a 'social mistake,' like spilling a drink at a social gathering. The experience usually reveals that people are more forgiving than assumed, which can alleviate some of the social anxiety.

3. Perfectionism: For a client whose perfectionism is hindering progress, ask them to intentionally make a minor mistake in their work and to observe what happens. Often, they'll find that the sky doesn't fall, and this can be a stepping stone toward more balanced behavior.

Paradoxical intention can seem like a risky technique due to its counterintuitive nature, but when applied thoughtfully, it has the potential to break through significant barriers of resistance. It empowers clients to confront their fears head-on, often with liberating results.

Positive Confrontation

This is not a confrontation in the traditional sense. Instead, it's a strategy where the coach gently but firmly calls attention to the client's resistant behavior or language. The goal is to enable the client to recognize their resistance and to encourage dialogue about it. Positive confrontation could be as simple as saying, "I notice you've been quiet after I suggested that exercise. Is there something about it that bothers you?"

Exercises and Activities for Overcoming Resistance

1. Resistance Role-Play: Coach and client switch roles, allowing the client to be the coach and confront resistance. This enables the client to see their resistance from another perspective.
2. Barrier Breaker Worksheet: A worksheet with targeted questions that help the client identify their own resistance, the fears fueling it, and steps to overcome it.

As a coach, your job isn't to bulldoze resistance but to navigate it—turning roadblocks into stepping stones for growth and transformation.

CHAPTER 12

TECHNIQUES FOR EMOTIONAL SELF-REGULATION

In the realm of coaching, emotions play a central role. Helping clients navigate and manage their emotions is a critical aspect of fostering growth and facilitating change. This chapter zeroes in on techniques designed to assist clients in achieving emotional self-regulation—a skill that empowers them to effectively manage their emotional states and responses.

Understanding Emotional Self-Regulation

Emotional self-regulation is the capacity to identify, understand, and modulate one's emotional responses. It involves acknowledging emotions without being overwhelmed by them and choosing appropriate responses even in the face of challenging feelings. As coaches, teaching clients to regulate their emotions equips them with a valuable tool for navigating life's ups and downs.

Affirmations and Coping Statements

Affirmations and coping statements are powerful tools that can assist clients in shifting their mindset and managing their emotions. These techniques are designed to replace negative or self-defeating thoughts with positive and empowering beliefs, helping clients reframe their perspective and build emotional resilience.

Affirmations are positive statements that clients repeat to themselves to foster a more constructive self-perception. These statements challenge negative self-talk and reinforce desired qualities, behaviors, or outcomes. The repetition of affirmations can gradually reshape deeply ingrained beliefs and encourage more self-compassion.

How to Use Affirmations:

Effectively integrating affirmations into coaching involves a strategic approach to reshape clients' self-perception and transform negative thought patterns. By following these steps, you can help clients harness the full potential of affirmations:

Begin by recognizing the negative thought pattern or self-belief that you aim to address. Whether it's self-doubt, insecurity, or any other limiting belief, pinpoint the issue that requires attention.

Construct affirmations that directly challenge and replace the negative belief. Ensure that these statements are concise, positive, and framed in the present tense. Steer clear of using negations. Instead of saying, "I am not anxious," encourage the affirmation "I am calm and composed."

Encourage clients to repeat their chosen affirmations consistently throughout their day. They can say these affirmations aloud, write them down, or seamlessly integrate them into their daily routines.

Suggest to your clients that they visualize themselves fully embodying the qualities described in the affirmation. Visualization adds a layer of depth to the affirmation's impact by engaging their power of imagination and enhancing the process of positive transformation.

Coping Statements

Coping statements are practical and realistic responses that clients can use to manage stressful situations or negative emotions. These statements help individuals distance themselves from distressing thoughts and instead focus on constructive ways to handle challenges.

1. Identify Triggers: Help clients identify situations or thoughts that trigger negative emotions or anxiety.
2. Generate Responses: Collaboratively create coping statements that provide reassurance, perspective, and a sense of control. For instance, if a client is facing a challenge at work, a coping statement could be, "I am capable of handling this situation one step at a time."
3. Practice and Rehearse: Encourage clients to practice these coping statements during coaching sessions and in their daily lives. Role-playing scenarios with different coping statements can help build confidence in using them effectively.
4. Apply in Real Life: Coach clients to apply these coping statements in real-life situations. When confronted with stressors, encourage them to recall and recite the coping statements to manage their emotions and responses.

Guided Visualization

Guided visualization is a technique that involves leading clients through a scripted mental journey to evoke positive emotions, enhance relaxation, and visualize their desired outcomes. This technique taps into the power of imagination to create a sensory-rich experience that can impact emotions and behaviors.

1. Create a Relaxing Environment: Ensure your client is in a quiet and comfortable space. Dim the lights, play calming music if desired, and guide them to close their eyes.
2. Set the Scene: Begin by describing a peaceful and serene setting. This could be a beach, a forest, or any place where your client feels at ease.
3. Engage the Senses: As you narrate the journey, incorporate sensory details. Describe the sights, sounds, smells, and textures they might encounter in this imagined environment.
4. Introduce the Goal: Guide your client to visualize achieving a specific goal or overcoming a challenge. Encourage them to vividly imagine the details of this achievement.
5. Positive Emotions: Prompt your client to explore the positive emotions associated with their success. Have them focus on the sensations of joy, satisfaction, and accomplishment.
6. Return to Reality: Slowly guide your client back to their present state, ensuring they feel grounded and refreshed.

Guided visualization is a valuable tool for managing emotions, reducing stress, and enhancing motivation. By leading clients through positive mental scenarios, you enable them to experience desired outcomes and emotional states, making it easier for them to navigate challenges and pursue their goals.

CHAPTER 13

GROUP COACHING TECHNIQUES

Creating a successful group coaching experience doesn't happen by accident. It requires a well-thought-out strategy, starting with defining clear goals and objectives and establishing a welcoming, open environment for all participants. In this section, we will delve into these crucial preliminary steps that set the tone for your entire group coaching series.

Importance of Defining Goals and Objectives for the Group Coaching Series

Before you gather your participants for the first session, it's critical to establish what you aim to achieve. Goals and objectives serve as the North Star, guiding both the coach and the participants through the journey ahead. Are you targeting career development, personal growth, overcoming specific challenges, or a combination of these? Clear goals allow for a focused approach, making each session more productive.

Practical Steps:

- » **Consult Stakeholders**: If the group coaching is being done within an organizational context, consult stakeholders to align the coaching objectives with organizational goals.
- » **Pre-Assessment Surveys**: Conduct surveys or interviews with prospective participants to understand their individual goals and expectations. This can help you tailor the group objectives to better meet the needs of individual participants.
- » **Clarity and Specificity**: Make the objectives as clear and specific as possible. Ambiguous goals can lead to confusion and lack of direction.
- » **Communicate**: Clearly communicate these objectives in the first session and make sure they are visible and referred to throughout the series.

A group coaching session is an intimate setting where participants might be sharing personal experiences, challenges, and fears. It's imperative that everyone feels safe enough to open up and be honest in their communication. A secure environment enhances the level of engagement, allows for constructive feedback, and increases the chances of participants achieving their goals.

Understanding Group Dynamics

As you embark on your group coaching journey, one of the most crucial elements to master is the nuanced field of group dynamics. The essence of group dynamics lies in how individual personalities impact the collective behavior and performance of the group. Individual traits, communication styles, and behavior patterns can either synergize to create a harmonious, productive atmosphere or clash to create discord and inefficiency.

For instance, you may have an extroverted participant who is eager to share, and while this can energize the group, it can also overshadow more introverted members who may have valuable insights but are hesitant to speak up. On the flip side, more reserved individuals may provide a grounding energy, helping to deepen discussions by encouraging more reflective thinking. Therefore, striking a balance between various personality types is crucial for fostering a collaborative and enriching group environment.

So, how do we manage these disparate personalities to create harmony and encourage productive conversations? First, it's essential to have an initial assessment period where you observe the natural flow of interaction among group members. This observation allows you to pinpoint dominant traits, possible friction points, and the general mood of the group.

Next, employ structured activities designed to include all voices. Techniques like "round-robin," where each member gets a turn to speak, or using anonymous suggestion boxes for submitting questions and topics can provide platforms for quieter voices. Meanwhile, setting a timer for responses can help in keeping more dominant personalities in check.

It's also beneficial to openly discuss the importance of balanced participation and actively invite quieter members to share their thoughts, while diplomatically moderating more dominant speakers. Having private one-on-one conversations with participants who may need individualized guidance on group interaction can be incredibly helpful too.

Always remember, the goal is not to change individuals or to suppress their natural tendencies, but rather to guide the group in such a way that each member's strengths are utilized, and their weaknesses mitigated. This balanced approach not only leads to more productive conversations but also brings the group closer to achieving its collective goals.

By recognizing the impact of individual personalities and implementing strategies to manage them effectively, you can navigate the complexities of group dynamics, ensuring a cohesive, productive, and fulfilling group coaching experience for all involved.

Core Techniques for Group Coaching

Mastering the core techniques for group coaching is vital for any aspiring life coach aiming to create impactful, effective sessions that benefit all participants. Each technique serves a unique purpose and can be adapted depending on the particular needs and dynamics of your group. Below, we delve into some of the most effective techniques to enrich your group coaching repertoire.

Socratic Questioning

One of the hallmarks of skilled coaching is the ability to ask questions that provoke thought, elicit responses, and engage participants in deep self-reflection. The technique of Socratic Questioning involves asking open-ended, leading questions that challenge individuals to think critically. In a group setting, this can lead to enlightening conversations that inspire collective wisdom and personal insights.

Facilitation Skills

Managing a group requires the deft skill of facilitation to keep the discussion on topic, engage all participants, and manage time effectively. Skilled facilitators know when to step in and steer the conversation and when to step back to allow organic discussion. Keep an eye on participants who may be disengaged and find ways to involve them, ensuring that the group reaps the benefits of diverse perspectives.

The "Hot Seat" Technique

This method focuses on one participant's specific issue, challenge, or goal while the rest of the group listens and later offers feedback or shares similar experiences. This technique allows for deep dives into individual issues while providing collective insights. It creates a sense of shared journey, making the session impactful not just for the person in the "hot seat" but for the entire group.

Fishbowl Technique

In the Fishbowl Technique, a participant volunteers to share a problem or question while the rest of the group acts as observers. After the participant shares, the group offers feedback, perspectives, or potential solutions. This technique can be especially useful for tackling complex issues that benefit from multiple viewpoints.

SWOT Analysis

A SWOT Analysis—identifying Strengths, Weaknesses, Opportunities, and Threats—can be a dynamic group activity to engage participants in collective problem-solving or goal-setting.

By involving everyone in analyzing these elements, you can create a comprehensive picture that aids in decision-making and planning.

By mastering these core techniques, you equip yourself with the tools to make your group coaching sessions as effective as possible. Each method offers unique benefits and can be used in different combinations to meet the specific needs and objectives of your group. Skillful application of these techniques can significantly elevate the group coaching experience, leading to meaningful transformations and the achievement of collective goals.

Case Studies: Real-World Examples of Effective Group Coaching Techniques

Understanding theory and techniques is one thing, but seeing them in action provides a different level of insight. Below are some real-world case studies that highlight effective group coaching techniques in various settings, demonstrating the impact these methods can have.

Case Study 1: Corporate Leadership Development

Technique Used: Fishbowl Technique

Outcome: Improved Interdepartmental Communication

In a tech company struggling with siloed departments, an executive coach used the Fishbowl Technique to address communication issues. Members from different departments sat in a circle and discussed a project they had collaborated on, while others observed. The observers noted communication bottlenecks and offered solutions. Within months, interdepartmental communication improved significantly, leading to more efficient project completion times.

Case Study 2: Career Transition Group

Technique Used: Socratic Questioning

Outcome: Clarity in Career Goals

In a group coaching session for professionals considering a career change, the coach used Socratic Questioning to help participants examine their motivations, strengths, and challenges. This introspective dialogue led many participants to realize their true career aspirations, and some even decided to take concrete steps such as enrolling in relevant courses or reaching out to mentors in their desired field.

Case Study 3: Mental Wellness Community Group

Technique Used: "Hot Seat" Technique

Outcome: Enhanced Emotional Well-being

A mental wellness coach running community group sessions focused each meeting on one participant's particular struggle, using the "Hot Seat" Technique. Other group members offered support and shared personal stories and coping strategies. Over the course of several sessions, participants reported feeling more equipped to manage their emotional challenges.

Case Study 4: Tcam Building in Non-Profit Organizations

Technique Used: SWOT Analysis

Outcome: Increased Fundraising Capabilities

A group coach working with a non-profit organization employed SWOT Analysis to assess their fundraising capabilities. This involved all team members and led to a collective understanding of the organization's Strengths, Weaknesses, Opportunities, and Threats in this area. Armed with these insights, the organization was able to design a more effective fundraising strategy that led to a 30% increase in donations within the next quarter.

Case Study 5: Online Entrepreneur Mastermind Group

Technique Used: Facilitation Skills

Outcome: Business Growth

An online group of aspiring entrepreneurs met weekly under the guidance of a business coach. Utilizing excellent facilitation skills, the coach managed to balance participation among the extroverted, naturally vocal members, and the quieter, more introverted members. As a result, the group benefitted from diverse perspectives, which led to innovative solutions and business growth for multiple members.

These case studies demonstrate the transformative power of effective group coaching techniques when applied thoughtfully and strategically. Whether you're coaching a corporate team, guiding a community group, or leading a mastermind of ambitious individuals, the right techniques can make all the difference.

CHAPTER 14

THE SMART MODEL – ADVANCED

In the realm of goal-setting and personal development, the SMART model has been a cornerstone, offering a straightforward framework for individuals and organizations to articulate and pursue their objectives. While the basic model—emphasizing Specific, Measurable, Achievable, Relevant, and Time-bound goals—has proven invaluable, there are complexities and nuances often not covered in its introductory layers. This chapter aims to delve into an advanced understanding of the SMART model, exploring its depth and breadth to navigate intricate goal landscapes more effectively.

But why do we need an advanced approach to a model that is appreciated for its simplicity? The reason is that goals are not static; they evolve as we navigate through life's complexities and as we grow both personally and professionally. Simple goals may work well for short-term tasks or individual projects, but for multifaceted objectives, long-term aspirations, or team-based initiatives, a more nuanced approach is necessary.

In the forthcoming sections, we will revisit each element of the SMART acronym, adding layers of complexity and detail to suit advanced scenarios. We will also expand the model to include two more pillars—Evaluation and Review—transforming it into the SMARTER framework. Real-world case studies will provide tangible examples of how these advanced techniques have been effectively employed, while discussions on digital tools and potential pitfalls will equip you with a comprehensive skill set for advanced goal-setting.

Whether you're a seasoned coach looking to deepen your methodology, a team leader aiming for organized success, or an individual yearning for personal growth, this chapter will offer valuable insights and actionable strategies for elevated goal-setting. Prepare to engage with the SMART model like never before, enriching both your practice and your life's pursuits.

The SMART model

As you've no doubt encountered, the SMART model is an acronym standing for Specific, Measurable, Achievable, Relevant, and Time-bound. While these elements are commonly understood in a general sense, an advanced understanding of each can make the difference between a goal merely set and a goal successfully attained. Let's revisit these critical elements one by one, peeling back the layers to delve into their more intricate applications.

Specific: The Importance of Clarity

Traditionally, "specific" simply meant not being vague— setting a goal to "lose weight" should instead be "lose 15 pounds." However, in an advanced context, specificity involves not just what the goal is but also how it connects to larger life or organizational themes. Being specific means aligning the goal with a broader vision, including specifying the resources needed, the steps to be taken, and the milestones to be achieved along the way.

Measurable: Advanced Metrics

Measurability ensures that progress can be tracked, typically by converting aspects of the goal into quantifiable units like time, percentages, or amounts. But what about goals related to softer skills like leadership or emotional intelligence? Here, advanced metrics come into play—competency assessments, 360-degree reviews, or even self-reflection journals that track behavioral changes over time. These qualitative metrics provide depth to the "Measurable" aspect of SMART goals.

Achievable: The Psychology of Feasibility

Aiming for the stars is wonderful, but the objective must also be realistically achievable to sustain motivation and commitment. In a more nuanced understanding of "Achievable," we also consider the psychological aspects of goal-setting. How does this goal make you feel? Anxious? Excited? The emotional resonance of a goal can affect its achievability, requiring coaches to be attuned to both their own and their clients' emotional landscapes.

Relevant: Alignment with Core Values

Being relevant not only means that the goal should make logical sense in the grander scheme of your life or organizational objectives, but it should also align with core values and beliefs. A "Relevant" goal resonates deeply, producing intrinsic motivation that can sustain you through the inevitable challenges and setbacks that come with pursuing any worthwhile objective.

Time-bound: Managing Deadlines in Complex Scenarios

A timeline creates urgency, but life is complicated, and projects often experience delays. Advanced SMART goals factor in such contingencies. For example, instead of a hard deadline, you might set a "soft" deadline with a two-week buffer period. Or you could establish phased deadlines for sub-tasks, allowing for adjustments without jeopardizing the overarching timeline.

Expanding to SMARTER Goals

As the landscape of goal-setting matures, so too does our understanding of the mechanisms that drive successful outcomes. While the SMART framework offers a solid foundation for setting meaningful objectives, evolving challenges demand an evolved framework. Enter the SMARTER model, which enhances the original by introducing two pivotal components: Evaluated and Reviewed. Together, these additions ensure that our goals remain dynamic and aligned with our ever-changing environments and aspirations.

Evaluated: Life is a series of events, changes, and new information. As we journey towards our goals, it's essential to periodically evaluate our progress, not just in terms of measurable outcomes, but in terms of relevance and alignment. Has a significant life event altered our priorities? Does the goal still align with our broader aspirations or the direction in which our profession is moving? Evaluating our goals in the light of new data ensures that we remain not only on track but on the right track.

Reviewed: Reflection has always been a powerful tool in personal and professional growth. Reviewing our goals means taking a step back and looking at the bigger picture, asking ourselves critical questions. What did we learn during the process?

Were there unforeseen obstacles, and how did we navigate them? This introspective process serves a dual purpose: it allows us to celebrate our successes, no matter how small, and to recalibrate our approach, ensuring that our methods are as effective as they can be.

Integrating these two elements into our goal-setting process ensures that our objectives are not static but living aspirations that adapt and grow as we do. The SMARTER framework recognizes the dynamism of life and the need for goals to be flexible and resilient. By evaluating our paths and reviewing our processes, we ensure that our goals are not only attainable but that they also truly resonate with our evolving selves.

In the realm of advanced goal-setting, the SMARTER model stands as a beacon, guiding us towards objectives that are not just smart in definition but astute in their ability to lead us towards genuine growth and fulfillment.

Case Studies: Advanced SMART Goals in Practice

Real-world examples are instrumental in understanding the applicability of any model. In the context of the advanced SMART goals, let's examine two compelling case studies that focus on personal development.

Case Study 1: Sarah's Journey to Emotional Resilience

Background: Sarah, a 32-year-old marketing manager, found herself struggling to cope with the emotional toll of her high-stress job. Her goal was to develop emotional resilience to better manage stress.

SMARTER Goal: To build emotional resilience by dedicating 15 minutes daily to mindfulness exercises for 90 days, with bi-weekly self-assessment check-ins, aligning with her long-term aspiration for well-rounded personal development.

Specific: The goal targeted emotional resilience and identified mindfulness exercises as the method.

Measurable: Success was quantified as completing 15-minute sessions for 90 days.

Achievable: Given her busy lifestyle, 15 minutes a day was a realistic commitment.

Relevant: The goal aligned with her broader life aspiration of being emotionally balanced.

Time-bound: The 90-day period provided a clear timeframe.

Evaluated: Sarah conducted bi-weekly self-assessments to evaluate her progress and emotional state.

Reviewed: After the 90-day period, Sarah reflected on her journey, celebrating her successes and recalibrating her approach for future goals.

Outcome: At the end of the 90 days, Sarah reported feeling more resilient and better equipped to manage work-related stress. Her success with this goal motivated her to integrate mindfulness as a long-term practice.

Case Study 2: Tom's Quest for Professional Advancement

Background: Tom, a 45-year-old sales executive, wanted to move into a managerial role but lacked some of the required skill sets, such as team leadership and budget management.

SMARTER Goal: To acquire the skills needed for a managerial role by completing three industry-certified courses in leadership and financial management within the next six months, while also seeking feedback from supervisors.

Specific: Tom identified the skills he needed and chose industry-certified courses as the way to acquire them.

Measurable: The completion of three courses served as the metric for success.

Achievable: Given his work schedule and personal commitments, Tom found the goal to be achievable.

Relevant: The goal was directly related to his career advancement.

Time-bound: A six-month timeframe provided urgency yet allowed adequate time for completion.

Evaluated: Tom sought monthly feedback from his supervisors to assess how well he was integrating his new skills into his job.

Reviewed: At the end of six months, Tom reviewed his progress, celebrating his course completions and the positive feedback received.

Outcome: Tom successfully completed all three courses within the stipulated time and received commendable feedback from his supervisors. His newly acquired skills made him a strong contender for upcoming managerial roles in his organization.

These case studies exemplify how the SMARTER model can be implemented effectively in real-world scenarios, particularly for personal development goals. They demonstrate the importance of each element of the model and how they contribute to the ultimate success of the individual's aspirations.

Common Pitfalls and How to Overcome Them

Even the most robust models like SMART are not immune to misapplication, and life coaches often encounter pitfalls that can hinder the effectiveness of the goals they set with their clients. Understanding these pitfalls can guide us in setting not just any goals, but truly impactful ones.

One common trap is the overemphasis on measurability, sometimes at the expense of the qualitative aspects of a goal. While it's essential to have metrics, reducing complex life goals to mere numbers can result in a loss of personal meaning and emotional engagement. This pitfall can be overcome by incorporating qualitative indicators such as self-assessments, peer reviews, or reflective journals that provide a more comprehensive picture of progress.

Another common error is the setting of overly ambitious, or conversely, overly conservative goals. An unrealistic goal can overwhelm, demotivate, and set up the client for failure. Conversely, a goal that's too easy may offer quick wins but ultimately fails to inspire or bring about meaningful change. To strike a balance, coaches should guide clients through a thorough assessment of their resources, constraints, and past performance before settling on what is truly "Achievable."

Similarly, coaches may forget the "Relevant" component, setting goals that may seem valuable on the surface but lack alignment with the client's core values or long-term objectives. Such goals can lead to short-lived satisfaction but eventually result in a sense of aimlessness. To avoid this, spend ample time discussing the client's broader life vision, ensuring that the SMART goal is a stepping stone along that larger path.

The "Time-bound" element can also be a double-edged sword. While deadlines create a sense of urgency, they can also induce undue stress, especially if they are unrealistic or inflexible. Coaches should aim for timeframes that are challenging yet reasonable and be prepared to adjust them in response to unforeseen circumstances or challenges.

Moreover, the failure to periodically evaluate and review the goals—extensions provided by the SMARTER model—can also cause challenges. Goals set in stone can become obsolete as life situations change, so the regular evaluation and review can keep the objectives aligned with evolving needs and circumstances.

By being aware of these common pitfalls and employing strategies to navigate around them, life coaches can harness the true power of the SMART model to deliver tangible and transformative results for their clients.

Integration with Other Coaching Models - How SMART Interacts with GROW, CLEAR

In the world of coaching, there are several other renowned models that practitioners frequently employ, such as GROW (Goal, Reality, Options, Will) and CLEAR (Collaborative, Limited, Emotional, Appreciable, Refinable). Understanding how SMART can be integrated with these other models can enrich your coaching toolbox and offer a more nuanced approach to facilitating client growth.

SMART and GROW

The GROW model provides a structured conversation flow that naturally accommodates the specifics of a SMART goal. When using GROW, the initial 'Goal' phase can be greatly enhanced by applying the SMART criteria to define the objective in a more comprehensive manner. As you move to the 'Reality' phase, you can bring in the 'Achievable' and 'Relevant' aspects of SMART to assess the client's current status and resources. Finally, in the 'Options' and 'Will' phases, the 'Time-bound' characteristic of SMART can add urgency and a definitive timeframe, guiding the client in creating a concrete action plan.

SMART and CLEAR

The CLEAR model emphasizes the emotional and relational aspects of goal-setting, which sometimes can be overlooked in the rigidly structured SMART model. When combining SMART with CLEAR, begin by setting a Collaborative goal that also meets the SMART criteria. This ensures that the goal is not just specific and measurable but also aligned with the client's emotional needs and interpersonal relationships. In the 'Limited' and 'Appreciable' steps of CLEAR, blend in the 'Achievable' and 'Relevant' aspects of SMART to make sure the goal is realistic and aligned with larger life objectives. Lastly, 'Emotional' aspects from CLEAR can be periodically Evaluated in the SMARTER model's evaluation phase, offering a more holistic view of progress.

By skillfully integrating the SMART model with GROW and CLEAR, coaches can offer a more dynamic and comprehensive approach to goal-setting. This fusion not only enhances the depth of the coaching conversation but also provides a robust framework that accommodates both the logical and emotional dimensions of human aspiration. Clients thereby benefit from a balanced and enriched coaching experience that caters to their diverse needs and facilitates meaningful, lasting change.

SMART Worksheet

SMART Goal Worksheet can be an incredibly useful tool for life coaches and their clients to outline, define, and track goals effectively. Here's a sample worksheet template that you might find helpful:

Client's Name: _________________________________

Date: ____

Goal Description

Write a brief description of the overall goal:

____

____

Specific

What specific outcomes do you want to achieve?

1. ____

2. ____

3. ____

Measurable

How will you measure success? List the metrics or indicators you'll use:

1. ____

2. ____

3. ____

Achievable

What steps or tasks are needed to achieve this goal?

1. ____

2. ____

3. ____

What resources will you need?

1. ____

2. ____

3. ____

Relevant

How does this goal align with your broader objectives or life vision?

____

____

Time-bound

What is your timeframe for achieving this goal?

Start Date: _______________________________________

End Date: _______________________________________

Milestones:

1. First Milestone (Date: _______________)

2. Second Milestone (Date: _______________)

3. Final Milestone (Date: _______________)

Evaluation

How often will you evaluate your progress?

- [ ] Weekly

- [ ] Bi-weekly

- [ ] Monthly

- [ ] Other: _______________________________________

Review

Date for Review: _________________

What will be the indicators to revise or adapt the goal?

1. ____

2. ____

3. ____

This worksheet is designed to guide the client through the SMART goal-setting process, ensuring that each aspect is thoroughly considered. It also incorporates the elements of the SMARTER model, allowing for ongoing evaluation and review. Feel free to adapt it to your specific coaching needs!

PART V

ETHICS AND BOUNDARIES

CHAPTER 15

THE IMPORTANCE OF ETHICS IN COACHING

Life coaching is a profession that thrives on the sacred trust established between the coach and the client. In a landscape where personal dreams, fears, and vulnerabilities are laid bare, the ethical framework of the coaching relationship becomes non-negotiable. At the crux of this ethical edifice lies the principle of confidentiality—a cornerstone that upholds the integrity, professionalism, and effectiveness of the coaching endeavor. This article aims to elucidate the profound importance of ethics, focusing particularly on the element of confidentiality, and offers practical guidelines for life coaches.

In any professional setting, ethics are the moral principles that govern behavior. In the life coaching context, these ethical considerations become exponentially significant, considering the intimate, deeply personal nature of the relationship. Ethical conduct in coaching safeguards both parties and fortifies the core objective: meaningful, measurable personal growth for the client. The absence of ethics can lead to malpractice, loss of credibility, and a potential failure in helping clients achieve their goals.

Moreover, it taints the entire coaching industry, devaluing the contributions of countless professionals who operate with integrity and honor.

Confidentiality is often the first promise made in the coaching relationship and for good reason. It allows the client to feel secure, opening the gateway for honest and transparent dialogue. In the absence of guaranteed confidentiality, the client may hold back essential information, significantly undermining the effectiveness of the coaching relationship.

Guidelines for Maintaining Confidentiality

Knowing the importance is the first step, implementing it effectively is the crux of ethical practice. Here are some guidelines to navigate the complex terrain of confidentiality:

1. Explicit Agreements: At the onset of the coaching relationship, explicitly outline the terms of confidentiality. Make sure that your client knows what will be kept confidential and what won't be.
2. Secure Storage: All notes, voice recordings, or any other form of information collected during sessions should be securely stored. This could mean password-protected digital files or a secure physical storage system.
3. Limited Sharing: Under no circumstances should client information be shared with third parties unless explicitly agreed upon, or in scenarios where there might be risk of harm to the client or others.
4. Consultation Scenarios: If you consult with peers or supervisors for coaching advice, ensure that the client's identity is kept anonymous to maintain confidentiality.

5. Digital Platforms: If you are using digital tools for sessions, make sure they are encrypted and compliant with privacy laws.
6. Legal Exceptions: Be aware that legal scenarios like subpoenas can force the revelation of confidential information. In such cases, it's crucial to consult legal advice and communicate transparently with the client.
7. Ongoing Dialogue: Keep the lines of communication open. If a situation arises where confidentiality might be compromised, discussing this proactively with the client is often the best approach.

Ethical considerations are not a side note in the coaching profession; they are the very fabric that holds it together. Among these, confidentiality is perhaps the most critical, serving as the bedrock upon which the edifice of trust and effectiveness is built. A breach in confidentiality doesn't just impact one client; it shakes the integrity of the coaching relationship and, by extension, the entire coaching industry. As guardians of personal growth and catalysts for transformation, life coaches have a moral and professional obligation to uphold the highest standards of ethics, with confidentiality at its core.

Avoiding Conflicts of Interest

Conflicts of interest in life coaching can emerge in many forms, each with the potential to compromise the integrity of the coaching relationship. From personal relationships and multiple roles to financial interests and organizational dynamics, these conflicts present ethical challenges. The key to avoiding these pitfalls lies in a multi-pronged approach rooted in transparency and ethical rigor.

Begin by disclosing any potential conflicts to your client; transparency is the cornerstone of trust. Support this by establishing a clear, written agreement that delineates the boundaries and expectations of the coaching relationship. If you find yourself wearing multiple hats, perhaps as a consultant and a coach for the same client, make sure you separate these roles clearly, reiterating their distinct boundaries to avoid any overlap or confusion.

In situations where a conflict is insurmountable or too compromising, the most ethical decision may be to decline or terminate the coaching engagement. In such cases, it's useful to have a referral network of other coaches who can take over. Financial transparency is another critical aspect; avoid having a financial stake in any decisions your client might make, or at the very least, disclose such interests openly.

Regular consultations with a professional supervisor can provide impartial guidance on how to navigate complex ethical scenarios, including conflicts of interest. And if you find yourself tempted to coach a close friend, family member, or someone in your organizational hierarchy, it's often best to steer clear. Personal relationships can cloud professional judgment, making it difficult to maintain an unbiased perspective.

By taking these comprehensive steps, life coaches can successfully navigate the intricate ethical landscape, thereby safeguarding the coaching relationship and upholding the broader ethical standards of the profession.

CHAPTER 16

MAINTAINING PROFESSIONAL BOUNDARIES

Life coaching is a symbiotic relationship that thrives on trust, mutual respect, and a well-defined scope of engagement. As a life coach, you hold a unique position of influence in someone's life. Your words, actions, and even your implied commitments can have a far-reaching impact on your clients. Thus, the importance of maintaining professional boundaries cannot be overstated. This chapter aims to delve into three critical aspects of professional boundaries: emotional boundaries, time boundaries, and the ethical considerations that encapsulate them both.

The concept of emotional boundaries in a life coaching relationship is complex and multifaceted. Let's delve deeper into this particular aspect.

Emotional Boundaries: Complex Web of Empathy and Professionalism

Life coaches often find themselves navigating a complex emotional landscape with their clients. The very nature of the role demands a deep level of understanding, compassion, and, most importantly, empathy. Clients come with a myriad of issues, hopes, dreams, and traumas. To effectively guide them toward their goals, a life coach must tap into this emotional reservoir in a way that is both sensitive and insightful.

The Double-Edged Sword of Empathy

Empathy, while an invaluable tool in the coaching arsenal, can also act as a double-edged sword. On one hand, empathy allows the coach to resonate with the client, offering invaluable emotional support. This level of understanding often leads to stronger trust, and a well-placed empathetic comment can be the catalyst for a significant breakthrough.

On the other hand, excessive empathy can distort the professional dynamic. When a coach becomes too emotionally invested in a client's life, the clarity of their role can become obscured. Emotional investment can cloud judgment, shift focus away from the client's goals, and make it challenging for the coach to offer impartial advice. There's also the risk of emotional exhaustion or "burnout" for the coach, which isn't just detrimental for the professional but also undermines the quality of support offered to the client.

The key here lies in balancing empathy with professionalism. The life coach must have the emotional acumen to connect deeply with the client while maintaining a level of detachment. This isn't to say the coach should be aloof or indifferent; rather, they should be deeply present, but not so emotionally entangled that their judgment becomes clouded.

Importance of Professional Context

This brings us back to the importance of the professional context of the relationship. At the end of the day, a life coach is hired for their professional skills, knowledge, and expertise. Emotional support is part of the package, but it is not the entire package. Coaches are not friends, therapists, or counselors. Their primary role is to help clients identify their goals, create actionable plans, and motivate them to achieve these goals.

Tactical Steps for Preserving Emotional Boundaries

1. Structured Communication: Use a structured format for each session that keeps discussions goal-oriented.
2. Check-ins: Periodically check in with yourself to assess if you're becoming emotionally entangled and take steps to recalibrate.
3. Peer Supervision: Engaging in peer supervision or mentorship can offer a 'second opinion' on maintaining appropriate emotional boundaries.
4. Self-Care: Practicing self-care ensures that you're emotionally equipped to handle your client's needs without jeopardizing your well-being.

Maintaining emotional boundaries while offering life coaching services is an ongoing process of self-awareness and professional development. Done well, it serves to elevate the coaching relationship, ensuring that it is both effective and ethically sound.

Failing to set these boundaries may result in an unhealthy emotional dependency, where the client perceives the coach as a friend or confidant rather than a professional guide. This could distract from the core objective of the coaching relationship: helping the client become self-reliant and achieve their goals.

Additional Tips for Maintaining Emotional Boundaries

1. Be Explicit: Make it clear from the onset what the coaching relationship entails and what it doesn't. Discuss the nature of the professional boundary in your initial sessions.
2. Non-disclosure: Respect the confidentiality of the information shared during coaching sessions. This not only protects the client but also prevents any emotional entanglements.
3. Avoid Overidentification: It's easy to find similarities between your experiences and those of your clients. While empathy is good, overidentification can lead to bias and compromised judgment.
4. Know When to Refer: If a client's emotional needs surpass your professional expertise, refer them to a qualified mental health professional.

Time Boundaries

Just as it's important to set emotional parameters, time boundaries are equally critical for maintaining a professional coaching relationship.

Your time is valuable, but so is your client's. Setting time boundaries, like punctuality and the duration of sessions, underscores professionalism and ensures that the coaching agenda stays on course.

Tips for Time Boundaries

1. Be Punctual: Arrive on time for sessions and expect the same from your client. Punctuality sets the tone for the entire coaching relationship.
2. Set Duration: Make sure the client is aware of the session duration and stick to it. Running over time can be interpreted as a lack of respect for the client's time.
3. Respect Off-hours: Clearly communicate your availability outside of scheduled sessions and stick to it. This reinforces professional boundaries and allows you to maintain your own work-life balance.

Ethical Considerations

Maintaining professional boundaries is not just about efficiency or focus; it's fundamentally an ethical issue. Ethical standards in life coaching are designed to protect both the client and the coach, ensuring the integrity of the profession.

1. Confidentiality: Upholding strict emotional boundaries inherently involves maintaining confidentiality, a key ethical consideration in any coaching relationship.
2. Non-exploitation: Abiding by time boundaries ensures you're not exploiting the client for additional time or billing.
3. Competence: Recognizing your limitations—be it emotional or time-related—and referring clients to other professionals when needed is an ethical obligation.
4. Professionalism: Adhering to professional boundaries underpins the ethical principle of professionalism, solidifying your credibility and the credibility of the coaching profession.

Maintaining professional boundaries isn't a mere checkbox in the list of coaching responsibilities. It's a nuanced, ongoing effort that deeply impacts the efficacy and integrity of your coaching practice. By adhering to clearly defined emotional and time boundaries, you not only create a conducive environment for your client's growth but also uphold the esteemed ethical standards that legitimize the coaching profession.

PART VI

EXTRA MATERIAL

Chapter 17

Setting Up Online Coaching Practice

Below is a breakdown of the technology needed to run an online coaching practice effectively.

Website

1. Domain Name & Hosting Your website is your business card, and it all starts with a domain name and reliable hosting.
2. Content Management System (CMS) Platforms like WordPress allow for flexibility and customization without requiring advanced coding skills.
3. SSL Certificate To secure transactions and personal information, an SSL certificate is crucial.

Online Session Platforms

1. Video Conferencing Tools Zoom, Skype, and Microsoft Teams are popular options. Look for features like recording capabilities, breakout rooms for group coaching, and good security measures.

2. Chat Platforms Messaging apps like Slack or even WhatsApp can serve as auxiliary channels for communication.

Appointment Scheduling

1. Scheduling Software Tools like Calendly, Acuity Scheduling, or Book Like A Boss allow clients to see your availability and book sessions without back-and-forth emails.
2. Calendar Integration Make sure your scheduling software integrates with your personal and business calendars to avoid double bookings.

Payment Processing

1. Payment Gateways PayPal, Stripe, and Square are commonly used. Ensure that they can be easily integrated into your website for seamless transactions.
2. Invoicing Software Apps like FreshBooks or QuickBooks can generate invoices and keep track of payments.

Customer Relationship Management (CRM)

1. Client Database Software like Salesforce or HubSpot CRM can help you track client interactions, notes from sessions, and other key client information.
2. Email Marketing Automate newsletters or follow-up emails with tools like Mailchimp or ConvertKit.

Online Surveys and Assessments

1. Tools like SurveyMonkey or Google Forms can help you gather pre-assessment information or post-session feedback. This data can guide the focus of your sessions

and give you insights into the group's progress and areas for improvement.

2. Virtual Whiteboards and Mind Mapping

3. Platforms like Miro or MURAL offer interactive, digital whiteboards that can be used for brainstorming, SWOT analyses, or real-time group activities. These can be particularly effective for visual learners and can also be saved for future reference.

Content Creation & Distribution

1. Screen Recording Software like Camtasia or OBS Studio for creating and sharing video content.
2. Document Sharing Google Drive or Dropbox for sharing resources, exercises, or reading materials.
3. Social Media Management Tools like Hootsuite or Buffer for managing multiple social media accounts.

Data Security

1. Firewall & Antivirus Ensure you have strong firewalls and antivirus software to protect both your and your clients' information.
2. Data Encryption Use VPNs and other encryption tools for added security.

Analytics

1. Website Analytics Google Analytics for tracking website visits, bounce rates, and other relevant metrics.
2. Customer Feedback Tools Consider using surveys and feedback tools to gauge client satisfaction and areas for improvement.

Having a solid technology stack is not just a convenience but a necessity for a modern online life coaching business. It adds a layer of professionalism, improves client interaction, and allows for scalable growth. By investing in the right technology, you can focus more on delivering high-quality coaching rather than dealing with administrative hassles.

CHAPTER 18

ONGOING LEARNING AND DEVELOPMENT

In the dynamic field of life coaching, standing still is akin to moving backward. The landscape is continually changing, influenced by scientific research, technological advancements, and societal shifts. This makes the need for ongoing learning and professional development not just a bonus, but a necessity. This chapter delves into why continuous education is crucial, what types of educational opportunities exist, and how you can leverage various platforms and networks to keep yourself updated and your coaching skills sharp.

The phrase "lifelong learning" is more than just a buzzword; it's a commitment to excellence and adaptability. As a life coach, you are entrusted with the responsibility of guiding people through complex life changes, and your advice needs to be rooted in up-to-date methodologies and evidence. Continuing education ensures that you stay relevant, confident, and effective in your practice, adding layers of depth to your existing skill set.

Formal education in the form of courses and workshops is an effective way to upgrade your capabilities systematically.

Institutions and organizations often offer specialized courses, ranging from improving communication skills to understanding human psychology at a deeper level. Workshops, often more focused and time-sensitive, can offer practical, hands-on experience in specific areas such as conflict resolution or cognitive behavioral techniques. Regularly attending such educational gatherings not only enhances your skills but also expands your professional network.

Peer Networks and their Benefits

Never underestimate the power of a robust professional network. Peer learning groups, coaching associations, and online forums provide platforms for open discussions, knowledge sharing, and even collaborative problem-solving. By actively participating in these communities, you get access to a range of perspectives and experiences that you might not encounter otherwise. These networks also serve as excellent sources for referrals, partnerships, and sometimes even friendships that enrich you both professionally and personally.

Utilizing Online Resources for Continuous Learning

In today's digital age, you don't have to look far to find resources for learning. Webinars, online courses, podcasts, and even YouTube channels devoted to life coaching can offer you fresh insights right from the comfort of your home or office. Websites and online journals often provide a treasure trove of articles, case studies, and research papers that can help you stay updated on the latest trends and scientific findings relevant to life coaching.

The path to becoming an accomplished life coach is not a destination but a journey—one that requires continuous curiosity, effort, and adaptation. Lifelong learning is not an option; it's a necessity that adds value to your practice and, by extension, to the lives of those you coach. By continually upgrading your skills through courses, workshops, peer networks, and digital resources, you not only uphold the integrity of your profession but also enrich the quality of guidance you provide to your clients.

In this fast-paced world, the best investment you can make is in your knowledge and skills. Let this chapter serve as your roadmap for ongoing professional development in the fascinating, ever-evolving field of life coaching.

CHAPTER 19

NETWORKING AND COMMUNITY

No man or woman is an island, especially in the field of life coaching. Engaging with a larger community isn't just about schmoozing at events or collecting business cards; it's about developing relationships that enrich your practice, offer opportunities for growth, and provide a support network of like-minded professionals. In this chapter, we'll explore the strategies and tools that can make you an active, beneficial participant in the broader coaching community.

Importance of Networking in Coaching Profession

Networking, in essence, is relationship-building. In the coaching profession, these relationships serve multiple purposes: they can be a source of referrals, offer collaborative opportunities, or even act as a sounding board for new ideas and techniques. Additionally, a strong network can provide you with access to resources and knowledge you may not have encountered on your own, elevating both your expertise and your practice. Simply put, networking isn't an optional activity—it's an integral part of your professional landscape.

Best Practices for Effective Networking

Networking is an art form that requires more than just an outgoing personality. Here are some best practices for effective networking:

1. Be Genuine: Authenticity is crucial. People can sense when you're only interested in what they can do for you, so aim to build relationships rather than simply accumulate contacts.
2. Listen More, Speak Less: Listening is a skill that coaches excel at, and it's just as crucial in networking. Take the time to understand the other person's perspective and needs.
3. Follow Up: A quick email or a call expressing gratitude after a meeting can go a long way in solidifying a relationship.
4. Add Value: Offer something of value—be it a piece of advice, a contact, or even a relevant article—before asking for something in return.
5. Keep Learning: Use your network as a resource for learning. Be curious and open to acquiring new knowledge or skills from the people you meet.

Leveraging Social Media for Community Engagement

In the digital age, your network isn't limited to who you can meet in person. Platforms like LinkedIn, Twitter, and even specialized coaching forums provide an expansive virtual stage for community engagement. However, social media requires a different etiquette:

1. Be Consistent but Not Overwhelming: Choose platforms where you can consistently contribute without spreading yourself too thin.
2. Engage, Don't Broadcast: Social media is a two-way street. Respond to comments, participate in discussions, and use the platform to build relationships rather than just as a megaphone for your views or services.
3. Showcase Your Expertise: Share articles, offer insights, and post relevant content that adds value to your followers and positions you as an expert in your field.
4. Be Respectful: Remember that social media is a public forum. Be mindful of your language and respectful of differing opinions.

Networking and community involvement are not merely peripheral aspects of a successful life coaching career; they are central to it. A robust professional network and an active presence within the community can offer resources, opportunities, and emotional support that are invaluable as you navigate the complexities of this profession. By being genuine in your interactions, proactive in your outreach, and mindful in your social media engagements, you can foster relationships that not only enrich you professionally but also contribute to your personal growth. This chapter is your blueprint for becoming a thriving, interconnected member of the life coaching community.

Afterword & Conclusion

If you've made it to this point, it means you're serious about taking the enriching, challenging, and deeply rewarding path to becoming a life coach.

The chapters in this book have guided you through the foundational theories, practical skills, ethical considerations, and business acumen needed for a successful coaching career. And, as the last section emphasized, this is a profession of ongoing growth and community engagement.

Life coaching is about more than just a paycheck or a title; it's about the potential for profound impact. Each client you guide brings a unique set of challenges, aspirations, and opportunities for transformative change. As a life coach, you serve as both a catalyst and a witness to these life-altering moments. It's a responsibility that demands the best of your skills, ethics, and heart.

However, this book is only the beginning. Your journey as a life coach will be filled with unexpected twists and turns, compelling success stories, and unavoidable challenges. Stay committed to lifelong learning, to ethical practice, and to the powerful art of helping people unlock their potential. Lean on the community of peers and mentors around you; they are invaluable sources of wisdom and support.

Next Steps…

As you turn this last page, consider it the first step on your new path. Whether you are preparing for your certification exam, setting up your first coaching session, or even refining your practice based on years of experience, never stop elevating your craft. The resources and strategies outlined here are tools to keep sharpening.

You've Got This!

Becoming a skilled life coach won't happen overnight. But with dedication, compassion, and a solid foundation of knowledge and skills, you will make a difference in people's lives. And that, in the end, is the true measure of success.

Thank you for allowing this book to be a steppingstone on your journey toward becoming a life coach. We can't wait to hear about the incredible impact you'll make.

www.ingramcontent.com/pod-product-compliance
Lightning Source LLC
Chambersburg PA
CBHW050523160726

48003CB00001B/430